H. Dieter Heinen (Ed.)

The Kanobo Cult of the Warao Amerindians of the Central Orinoco Delta: The Nahanamu Sago Ritual

Ethnologische Studien

herausgegeben von

Ulrich Köhler

Institut für Völkerkunde
der
Albert-Ludwigs-Universität
Freiburg

Lit

H. Dieter Heinen (Ed.)

The Kanobo Cult of the Warao Amerindians of the Central Orinoco Delta: The Nahanamu Sago Ritual

Ethnologische Studien Bd. 41

Lit

Cover Picture: Performance of the *wahi arokohotu* in front of the *hebu ahanoko*.
Note the full moon rising in the east (Fig. 9 on page 13)

With editorial assistance by Nuria Martin and financial support by Total de Venezuela, Program LOCTI

Bibliographic information published by the Deutsche Nationalbibliothek
The Deutsche Nationalbibliothek lists this publication in the Deutsche Nationalbibliografie; detailed bibliographic data are available in the Internet at http://dnb.d-nb.de.

ISBN 978-3-643-90003-6

A catalogue record for this book is available from the British Library

Dufourstr. 31
CH-8008 Zürich
Tel. +41 (0) 44-251 75 05
Fax +41 (0) 44-251 75 06
e-Mail: zuerich@lit-verlag.ch
http://www.lit-verlag.ch

LIT VERLAG Dr. W. Hopf
Berlin 2009
Fresnostr. 2
D-48159 Münster
Tel. +49 (0) 2 51-620 32 22
Fax +49 (0) 2 51-922 60 99
e-Mail: lit@lit-verlag.de
http://www.lit-verlag.de

Distribution:

In Germany: LIT Verlag Fresnostr. 2, D-48159 Münster
Tel. +49 (0) 2 51-620 32 22, Fax +49 (0) 2 51-922 60 99, e-Mail: vertrieb@lit-verlag.de

In Austria: Medienlogistik Pichler-ÖBZ GmbH & Co KG
IZ-NÖ, Süd, Straße 1, Objekt 34, A-2355 Wiener Neudorf
Tel. +43 (0) 22 36-63 53 52 90, Fax +43 (0) 22 36-63 53 52 43, e-Mail: mlo@medien-logistik.at

In Switzerland: B + M Buch- und Medienvertriebs AG
Hochstr. 357, CH-8200 Schaffhausen
Tel. +41 (0) 52-643 54 85, Fax +41 (0) 52-643 54 35, e-Mail: order@buch-medien.ch

Distributed in the UK by: Global Book Marketing, 99B Wallis Rd, London, E9 5LN
Phone: +44 (0) 20 8533 5800 – Fax: +44 (0) 1600 775 663
http://www.centralbooks.co.uk/html

Distributed in North America by:

Transaction Publishers
New Brunswick (U.S.A.) and London (U.K.)

Transaction Publishers
Rutgers University
35 Berrue Circle
Piscataway, NJ 08854

Phone: +1 (732) 445 - 2280
Fax: + 1 (732) 445 - 3138
for orders (U. S. only):
toll free (888) 999 - 6778
e-mail: orders@transactionpub.com

CONTENTS

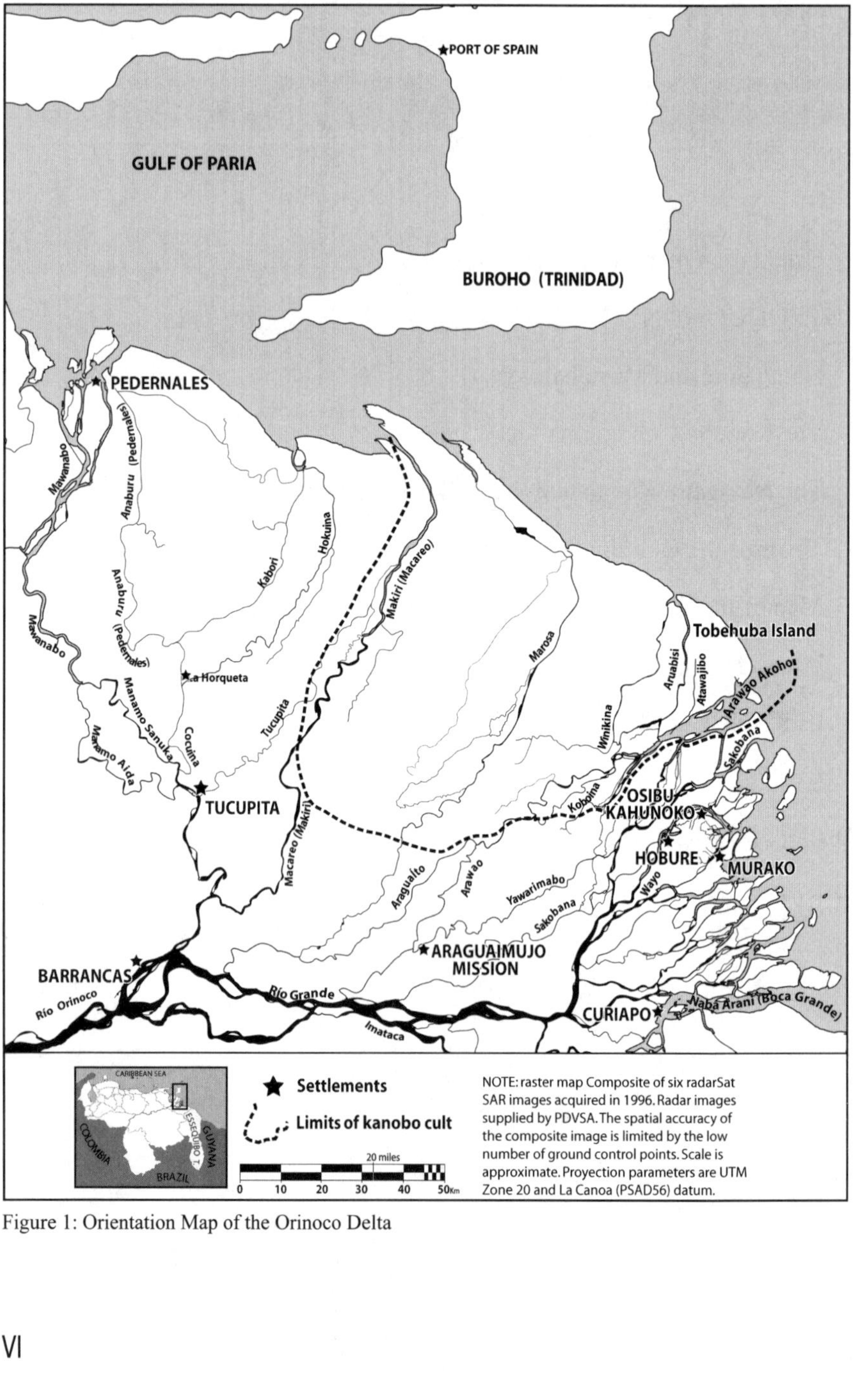

Figure 1: Orientation Map of the Orinoco Delta

INTRODUCTION

In 1974 Heinen and Ruddle published a paper in the Journal of Anthropological Research (formerly The Southwest Journal of Anthropology) on the Warao sago ritual (nahanamu) and the corresponding kanobo cult in the south-eastern area of the Central Orinoco Delta.([1]) Heinen at the time had witnessed some four nahanamu([2]) rituals, but we had no native report or detailed description of the dances and ceremonial activities involved. There was, however, a rather detailed sketch of the corresponding version of the sago ritual from the north-western area of the Central Orinoco Delta by Basilio M. de Barral (1964: 33-142). Here, Barral described what he called "las fiestas del Naja Namu o de Yajuna," the former term referring to the container made from moriche stalks and the latter referring to the unprocessed starch stored in the nahanamu container.

Then, in November of 1977, the late Antonio Lorenzano, a bahanarotu shaman from Morichi Sanuka in the Winikina River and good friend of Heinen, offered spontaneously a detailed narrative with the nahanamu as a principal topic. Over the years, Heinen had all details of the ritual explained by Warao friends and field assistants and had made transcriptions and preliminary translations of the narrative. But it turned out that Antonio's report ended abruptly with the imitation games of a number of fishes, birds and terrestrial animals at the end of the day. Missing was the very signifi-

---

[1] Heinen, H. Dieter & Kenneth Ruddle. 1974. Ecology, ritual, and economic organization in the distribution of palm starch among the Warao of the Orinoco Delta. Journal of Anthropological Research 30:116-138.

[2] For the transcription of Warao terms we used the official alphabet designed by the Venezuelan Department of Education, except for the /h/ sound, written as [j] in Venezuela.

Figure 2: Antonio Lorenzano Pacheco, "Idamo Kabuka"

cant chant of the howler monkey (wahi arokohotu), the prototype of Warao gerontocracy and the most solemn part of the ritual, because as a bahanarotu shaman Antonio did not know the chant which was the domain of a wisiratu-shaman.([3]) The two officiating shamans in the Winikina were Carlos Zapata and Isaías Rodríguez, now defunct half-brothers from the traditional Hebu Wabanoko village. As it turned out, this was an important circumstance as Carlos's son Paulino Zapata, himself a fledgling wisiratu-shaman, would help us to complete the report.

While Paulino was not quite advanced enough in his trade of wisiratu in order to be able to reproduce the text of the sacred chant of the howler monkey, he knew one of the few remaining masters, Federico Zambrano. In

[3] In the Central Delta some individuals pronounce the [d] allophone of the /r-d-l/ sound, e.g. wisidatu; in the western Delta the [r] allophone is pronounced consistently.

2004, Herrmann, at the time preparing a doctoral dissertation on the Western Orinoco Delta at the University of Tübingen, made a trip to the lower Central Delta and contacted Paulino, who took her to Federico Zambrano. Accordingly, we considered the text by Paulino as a transition, and continued with the chant by Federico Zambrano. The chant is sung in a secret shamanic language using mainly a Spanish and Carib vocabulary that a traditional Warao audience would hardly understand.([4]) In the end, however, we decided to insert a descriptive text by Antonio's grandson Segundo Rivero, who followed more the style of his grandfather than Paulino.

In the meantime we were also able to correct a number of ethnographic mistakes that had cropped up in the original article. There is first of all the correction of the meaning of the ethnonym Warao. While it is true that some Warao, especially in the Essequibo Territory but also in the original Siawani (Chaguanes) area of the western Delta, consider themselves navigators and are expert boat builders, the meaning in the Waraowitu ("true Warao") areas of the Central Delta is not "boat people" but "lowland people," corresponding as counterpart to hotarao, dry-land people or "criollos" (see Heinen et al. 1999: 24-25; see also Lavandero Pérez 1994: 17-21; for the interpretation by Barral see his "Los Indios Guaraúnos y su cancionero," 1964:1).([5]) The Siawani in colonial times also had villages in north-western Trinidad where today the town and river of Chaguanas is located, as well as the river Caroní (V.S. Naipaul, 2001 [1969]).([6])

Regarding the sago ritual nahanamu, the areas assigned in the pa-

[4] There is an ambiguity in the Warao language in that the term nokokitane has the meaning of :"to understand" but also "to hear." Accordingly, Segundo Rivero maintains that he understands (nokoya) the song of the howler monkey.

[5] As the Ataisiwari arao of Osibu Kahunoko, Murako, and Kwamuhu put it: Oko Warao, yatu hotarao. "We are Warao Indians, you are Tierra Firme people, Criollos."

[6] Heinen was informed early on by the late Toní Gómez, headman of Hubasuhuru village in the Arawao river that Warao means people of "terruños, playones," lowlands. Over many years, however, he has accepted the suggestion of colleagues that Warao is derived from wa(hibaka), "curiara," canoe and arao, people, a folk etymology going back at least to Sir Walter Roth ([1924] 1970).

per to the kanobo cult are indeed those of the ritual. In the western Delta along the Manamo (Mawanabo) and Pedernales (Anaburu) rivers there was in fact no trace of the ritual detected. Furthermore, the local Warao there do not consider themselves Waraowitu and contrast Warao with Kri'tianos, not with Hotarao.

In the south-eastern Delta south of the Merejina river, however, where the ritual is limited mainly to the nowara or communal meal (see Lavandero and Heinen 1986), the presence of kanobo stones was detected. The reason this was not noticed earlier was that people there referred to it vaguely as hoyo, "the stone" and no nahanamu ritual is performed. In Winikina as well as in the western area of the Central Delta, among the Nahoromo Warao, nowara is a communal meal of yuruma (ohidu aru) eaten with he crabs from July on, during the appearance of he ariawara, the origin of Cancer, the open cumulus Praesepe plus gamma and delta Cancri (Heinen & Lavandero, 1973, 35: 12-13).

As pointed out in the Heinen and Ruddle article of 1974, the exploitation of moriche (Mauritia flexuosa) palm starch is more uncertain in the Central Delta and requires storing of the sago or yuruma (ohidu aru) because the non-functional distributaries of the area become brackish during the dry season allowing mangroves to colonize the river banks. Consequently, the moriche palm groves are scattered widely across the swampy interior and during the months of June/July bottlenecks of food shortages occur (see also J. Wilbert 1996).

The ecological differences in the various Delta areas as well as the cultural and ritual distinctions between the south-eastern and the south-western Central Delta, however, merit some detailed comment because certain mistakes in the literature appear in this respect, some serious and some minor. This is the topic to which we now turn.

Navigators and Morichaleros([7])

We can assume that among the Warao there is a substratum of former seafood scavengers, whose range extended in pre-colonial times all along the South American northern coast. There are a number of indications that confirm this assumption, such as the note in Laurence Keymis'([8]) report, that the "Arwaos and Arrikarri spoke the Tiuitiuas' language" (Keymis, 1596).

Tiwi-tiwe is the criollo name for two subspecies of sandpipers (Tringa flavipes and Tringa melaneuca) whose names are derived from the Otomaco language of the middle Orinoco (Acosta Saignes 1961:106). According to Ralegh ([1596] 1986:108), Tiwi-tiwe was also used as a nickname for the Waraowitu and, erroneously, included the Siawani (see also Harcourt [1613] 1967:180). As reported by the better informed Spanish of Margarita Island, however, it was only applied to the former (the Waraowitu "true lowland people") but not to the Siawani (Chaguanes) who were more riparian .([9])

The Warao of Osibu Kahunoko (San Francisco de Guayo), returnees from the missions of the Catalan Capuchins located at the time upriver and to the south, continue to identify with these two types of related sandpipers and call them waharomu, playing with their ethnonym Waharao (see Lavandero and Heinen, 1986).

---

[7] Palm Grove Dwellers

[8] Captain Laurence Keymis (V.S. Naipaul's spelling) was Sir Walter Ralegh's associate and member of the latter's 1595 exploration up the Orinoco river to the mouth of the Caroní.

[9] We should not assume that there were more than two Waraoan speaking groups in the area in the late 16th century as the group known as Farautes (Waraotu) in today's Sucre and Monagas States in Venezuela were of the same type as the morichaleros. In fact, the captain of the Waraotu settlement of Warikén (Guariquén) told Heinen recently that the ethnonym stands really for Waraowitu. More than in the Delta, the canoes of the Waraotu at the village of Mosú are quite crude and these people are definitely Amerindians on foot.

There is also the occurrence of Warao place-names such as Amana, today's Mana River in French Guiana. Amana, perhaps the colonial name of what is today the so-called Caño Mánamo (Mawanabo in Warao)([10]), is a sure sign of a Warao presence such as the important Warao settlement of Uriabari on the left bank of the Orinoco in front of Ciudad Guayana and the mouth of the Caroní. There, the Orinoco River produces a side arm with the name of Amana. Uriabari is perhaps the Warao name for Baratubaro, according to Whitehead (1988) mentioned by Gonzalo Fernández de Oviedo.

All this agrees completely with the findings by the members of an ethno-ecological project carried on by the team of A. Hornborg at the University of Lund in Sweden (L. Eriksen, personal communication, 2006), who also confirm the contact of the Warao with the Carib speaking Ye'kwana, to which we return below.

Now, the Waraoan speaking Siawani (Chaguanes) were the people known as skilled makers of canoes, who navigated the waters of the Caribbean, leading to the folk-etymology of "canoe people" for all Warao, while it did not apply to the Waraowitu, the "Morichaleros" (palm grove dwellers) who occupied most of the refuge areas of the Orinoco Delta in early colonial times. The late Antonio Lorenzano, our friend and a native of the morichal settlement of Soburoho, told us that he was twelve years old before he ever set eyes on a dugout canoe. Nevertheless, he later became a skilled riparian carpenter during his bride service with the people of the Homini Sebe river, perhaps the descendants of a Siawani group.

Why is this important? It is important because most of the reports by early explorers on the Warao are made on the basis of visits to the settlements of Warao mixed with Carib and/or Arawak speakers along the main waterways, such as the descriptions of Warao villages by the Jesuit missionary José Gumilla in his famous "El Orinoco Ilustrado y Defendido" of 1741 (1963).

After the intrusions into important areas of the Orinoco Delta by these ethnic groups expanding on the basis of the manioc complex con-

---

[10] But, perhaps again, there could be a mix up with "La Horqueta," in colonial times a Spanish military post. Amana in Warao represents a river fork or bifurcation.

sisting of "sebucanes" (manioc presses), manioc graters, and "budares" (manioc griddles) together with sturdy dugout canoes some three thousand or so years ago, some of the choicest sections of the Delta were occupied by Warao mixed with or headed by Carib/Arawak horticulturists.([11]) The Waraowitu or morichaleros on the other hand pursue a yearly cycle of transhumance.

A parallel observation should be noticed: By the seventeenth century Arawaks and, more inland, Carib speakers, had replaced the Warao fo-

Figure 3: Marco Zapata, preparing for the Nahanamu Ritual, Winikina River (1960's) (Wilbert 1980: 102)

[11] The report by José Gumilla on his two trips to Warao settlements clearly indicates several important points: These Warao communities are in the Upper Delta close to the apex, probably on the Río Grande (this is substantiated by the "intolerable multitude of mosquitoes" and the division of the year into two six months segments, which does not apply to coastal areas); a Carib term, "murichi" is used for the moriche palm (Mauritia flexuosa, see Ruddle 1977) instead of the Warao term ohidu as well as the criollo term yuruma instead of ohidu aru for the palm starch; houses are covered with moriche leaves instead of with temiche as in the lower Delta; they are on piles but have walls: all indications of a Carib presence or leadership.

Figures 4: Observing the Nahanamu Ritual (Winikina River, 1960's)

ragers from many of the coastal areas. The Carib belt, in fact, reached all the way from what is today Venezuela to the Amazon and beyond. The identity of these Carib speakers also coincides over long stretches: the Wayano (or Oayana) are identical with the Paragotos ("people of the sea"), just as is the case with the Pariagoto and the Guayana of Sucre State in Venezuela([12])(see the maps by P. du Val d'Abbeville in Harcourt [1613] 1967 and Loukotka 1968: 201, 215).

[12] Only that here an /i/ has been inserted into the people's name and that of the adjacent Gulf of Paria due to a confusion as Columbus thought being in the East-Indies (Varela 1989: 233-4). In another paper Heinen has speculated that the Pariagoto (Paragoto) were the "Iguana people" (Gassón &Heinen 2008).

The Kanobo Cult among the Waraowitu

Before we come to our narrative on the Kanobo Cult we have to discuss the similarities and a few differences of the ritual among the Winikina from that of the Western Waraowitu, the (Aida) Nahoromo ("manatee eaters").

All Warao in the Winikina/Aruabisi area stress that one thing is the nahanamu ritual and another the habi sanuka dance. In fact, both Antonio Lorenzano and his grandson Segundo start their narrative putting emphasis on this aspect. One difference certainly is that the two rituals are presided over by two different specialists of Warao shamans: The wisiratu for the nahanamu on the one hand and the bahanarotu for the habi sanuka on the other.([13]) Among the Makiri arao Barral also includes the nowara. In Winikina, the nowara can be organized by any household head. This is certainly a question that should be researched further.

In both areas of the Central Orinoco Delta, east and west, the ritual is called the nahanamu and dedicated to the highest spirit hebu araobo. In both areas it is mentioned that this kanobo has a wife and family. Barral, however, mentions explicitly the mother of the hebu araobo which he names Yahuna.

All the nahanamu rituals Heinen has ever participated in contained sections of the habi sanuka ritual, So does the nahanamu as described by Suárez (1968). Antonio´s grandson Segundo, however, makes a distinction between these additions and the habi sanuka proper.

What the people on the Makiri river think, we don't know, but the nahanamu ritual proceeds there with equally important aspects of the habi sanuka ritual in them. Barral (1964) does not mention that these are different rituals.([14]) The habi sanuka is said to be celebrated with manioc tortillas (aru hota aru), but at the moment of performing certain aspects of it during the

[13] This is the situation observed in the present case; the Habi Sanuka is more a local affair and may be headed by any religious practitioner (Wisiratu, Bahanarotu, Kaidoko).

[14] He lists the habi sanuka scenes under the nahanamu heading (1964: 75-85).

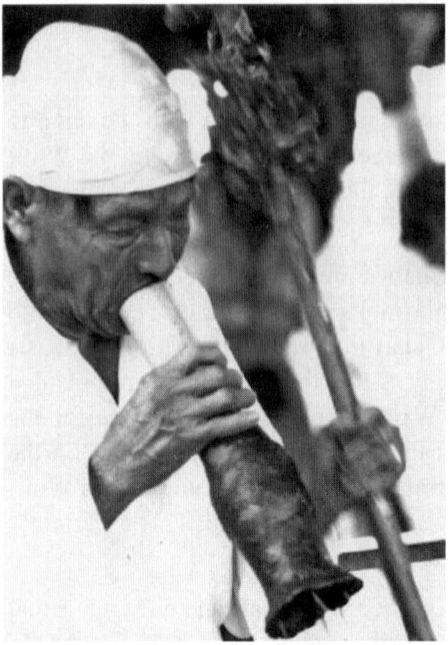

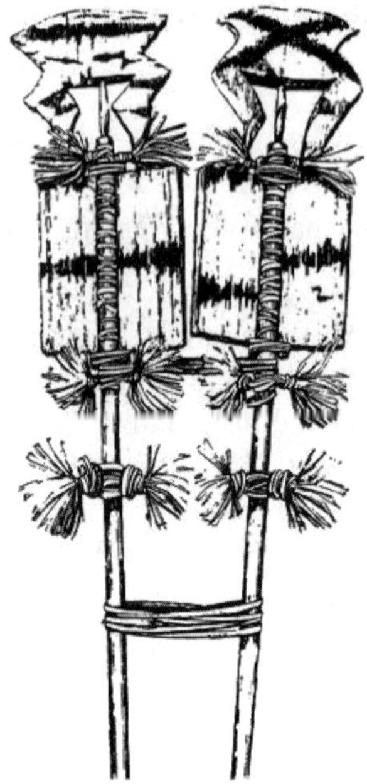

Figure 5: Charo of Koberuna village with isimoi clarinet

Figure 6: Female and male wooden daunona effigies (Wilbert 1972:112)

nahanamu the Winikinarao continue to feast on yuruma (ohidu aru). Barral points out that the habi sanuka reminds him of the Pemon parichara ritual (1964:7). We agree completely with his appreciation and it seems to us that equal similarity exists with the Ye'kwana wasaij jadü ritual, both important fertility dances. The reason for this will be discussed in the next chapter.

The Navigator Warao and the Ye'kwana/Lokono Connection

As was pointed out above, at the periphery of the Delta several groups of Amerindian horticulturalists had established themselves and partially mixed with the aboriginal Warao population.

What surprises students of the Warao Amerindians in the Orinoco Delta is the amount of Carib and Arawak terms, including with regard to the nahanamu ritual, but less so in the Central Delta among the morichaleros.

Figure 7: The ritual dance in front of the daunona effigies

Figure 8: Charo with *Hebu mataro* rattle

The closest Carib speakers to the Warao are the Kari'ña in the Sierra de Imataca just to the south. The connection with them is at hand, if only because they used to intrude into the Delta in search of fruits, notably during the pine-apple (anana) harvest. Furthermore, the definition of Warao as "navigators" probably originated in the area south of the Río Grande, in the area where Warao lived intermingled with the Arawak population along the coastal region to the east of the Delta coast (see the early colonial map of the "Aruacos," e.g. in Ojer, 1966).

Even if shamans and other religious practitioners traveled far and easily ranged into Carib speaking areas, the one place where we know of definite contact between the two ethnic groups is the large Warao settlement of Uriabari on the left hand shore of the Orinoco which was touched by a Ye'kwana trade route (L. Eriksen, pers. com. 2006). Accordingly, it could have resulted from contact with a Siawani (Chaguanas) group, the proverbial carpenters of robust dugout canoes (Ralegh [1596] 1848).

One of the instruments used during the nahanamu ritual is what is called in the criollo vernacular of the Delta "un botuto." In practice it refers,

Figure 9: Performance of the *wahi arokohotu* in front of the *hebu ahanoko*. Note the full moon rising in the east (Barral, 1964: 68)

however, to different instruments: among the morichaleros of the Winikina area it is applied to isimoi, a type of clarinet, while in the village of Bonoina in the Arawaimuhu ("Araguaimujo") river it is called wana, which means bamboo in the Ye'kwana language.([15])

Another Carib loan-word is sewei, the anklet worn during the habi sanuka([16]) celebration, particularly during the final phase of the daylight festivities called wayabaya ("closing"). The expression is derived from the Pemon term kewei (Barral 1964:52, 60). The Lokono (Arawak) term kareko, meaning the little quartz stones inserted into the hebu mataro rattle, is a loan-word from the Arawak language.

While some of the loan-words clearly prevail in the periphery of the Delta or among Warao groups in long-time contact with criollo populations, other terms are thoroughly integrated into ritual use.

Towards the culmination of the nahanamu ritual

The core of the nahanamu ritual starts with what Barral (1964: 57) terms "La Danza del Jatabu" (the dance of the arrows). These effigies of the Supreme Spirit in a female and a male version (1964: 58), are called in the Winikina area daunona, fashioned as among the Nahoromo from the board-like roots of the sangrito tree, a type of balsa wood.

The highlight of the nahanamu ritual, however, takes place after the "closing" of the festivities, at night-time, by the light of the full moon. What is common to the whole area of the kanobo ritual in the Central Delta, east and west, is the prayer for the children of the community to the hebu araobo, the supreme spirit, "el canto del kanobo." But there is a significant difference between the names of the chant. While in the Winikina it is called wahi arokotu ("the chant of the howler monkey") and is clearly targeted at the

---

[15] Even though the narrator does know the term wana (see below, # 113).

[16] As is obvious from the illustration in Barral (1964: 80), the atmosphere, with women and children roaming the hohonoko, is totally different from that of the wahi arokotu where young women and children are not allowed to be present.

Figure 10: Vision by 17th century Europe imagining the Warao living on trees during the rainy season, hoida (de Bry, 1612)([17])

Warao gerontocracy, including the huffing shout of the senior howler which makes everybody else fall silent, in the eastern part of the "Island of Mariusa" (in Warao Maresa), this phase of the ritual is called "La Oración Coral a Kuaimare" (the prayer to "the blessed one residing at the heights") (Barral, 1964: 35).([18]) Similar to both areas is, of course, the wording by Segundo Rivero: "wahi arokotu is the chant of the very kanobo, kanobo arokohotu," and the shout of the Makiriarao "kanobó" as the full moon appears over the

[17] This phenomenon actually is seen in the Upper Delta during the Orinoco River Flooding.

[18] Barral speaks also of "Nonatu" (or Creator)(1964: 36). This is, of course, part of the Warao syncretism as shown in the Warao expression: Kanonatu, Dioso, karani (Our creator, God, our mother)(Lavandero, 1986).

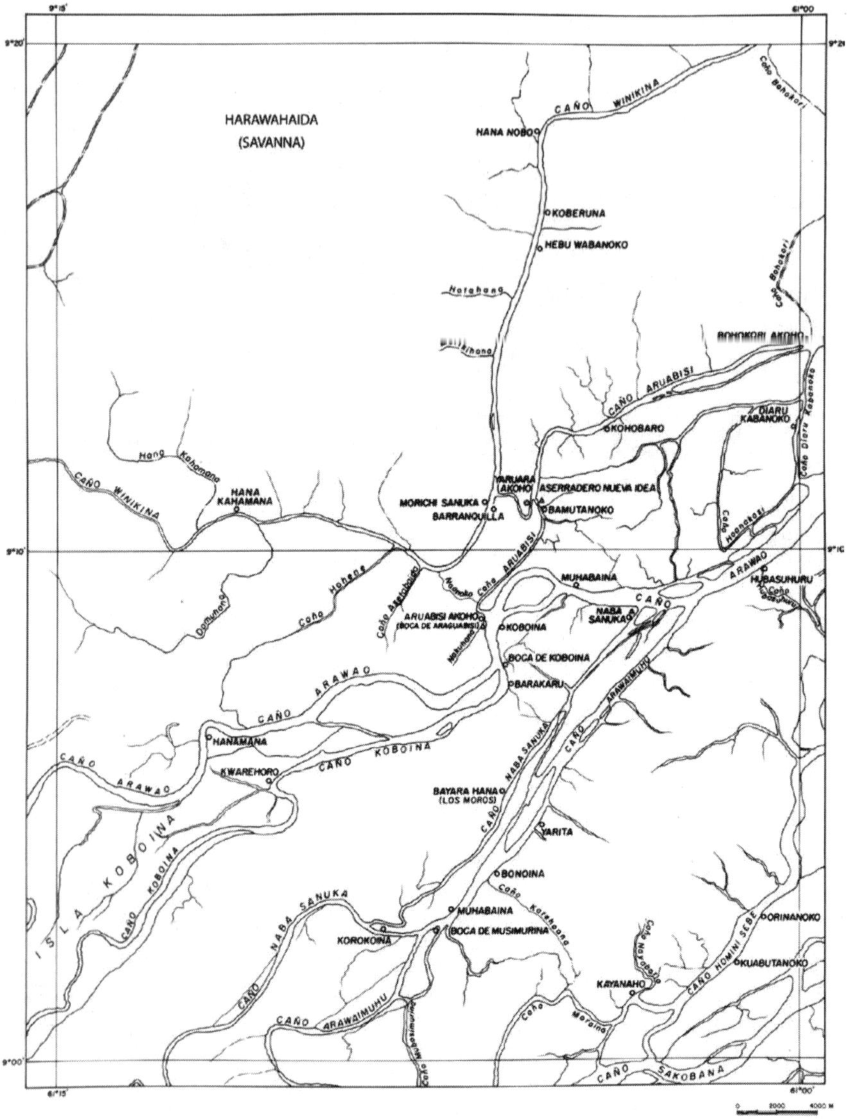

Figure 11: Map of the Winikina - Arawao - Naba Sanuka area

trees in the eastern sky (Barral 1964: 38, 69) in the night called waniku honi nakae ("when the moon fell into the water").

After the kanobo arokohotu (i.e. both the wahi arokotu and the kwaimare arokotu), the game of the howler monkey takes place. In the Winikina this is right after midnight while along the Makiri it is performed late at night, almost at dawn. We are still not quite sure what the relation to the animal games of the habi sanuka is.

Warao House Types in the Orinoco Delta

The shape of the Warao houses along the open Delta rivers constitutes an interesting construction of two independent frames inserted one into the other, a floor and a roof built on piles of mangrove trunks (see Suárez, 1968). The compound consists, as already pointed out by Barral (1964: 2-3), of hisabanoko, hanoko, y diawaranoko o nehemanoko, and in many traditional places, a kwaihanoko or hebu ahanoko (kitchen, living room/dormitory, and delivery-hut, as well as a hut for the shamans' equipment and the sacred kanobo stone).

This is an intermediate version of the poor huts, open to wind and rain, of the Warao in some of the south-eastern Delta areas where criollo traders established an encomienda type system, and the constructions of the Arawak families in San Francisco de Guayo or in the Amacuro, that boast next to a sturdy four-slope roof a bath hut over the river.

The huts of the morichal communities in turn are quite different, as they are built not on mangrove piles but on the stumps of felled and used moriche palms. They are quite small, about 3 by 4 meters large. The floors are fashioned from moriche bark, as is the dancing floor (hohonoko), resilient and flexible, between the huts of the community and the kwaihanoko to the east towards the rising moon, where the sago or "yuruma" (ohidu aru) is stored on the ground floor and where the wisiratu-shaman keeps his paraphernalia as well as the sacred stone, kanobo, above. Roofs are covered not with temiche leaves (yawihi), but with moriche (ohidu).

We are including the drawing presented by Barral (1964: 41, 68), as there are almost no photographs because of the difficulty to carry a camera miles over swampy terrain where one falls inevitably from the flimsy stems, meant to form a bridge, into the marsh.

Figure 12: Morichal village with cluster of huts, hohonoko dancing floor, and the hebu ahanoko in the east (Barral, 1964: 41)

The Nahanamu Ritual

narrated by Antonio Lorenzano on November 26th, 1977;

Morichi Sanuka, Winikina River; transcribed and translated with

Tirso Rivero, February 22nd – March 3rd, 1999.

1) *Nahanamu daisa, habi sanuka daisa. Nahanamu. Nahanamu abakitane obonohobuya. Ama tamatika ha tai Uboni.*

The nahanamu ritual is one thing, the habi sanuka dance another. Nahanamu.([1]) He is thinking of organizing a sago ritual. Now, here is this shaman Uboni, "the one that never sleeps."

2) *Tai ubaya, musubuya. Nahanamu. Kanobo nahanamu obonoya. Atae ubaya, musubuya. Kanobo tai awisitaya, aubataya.*

Uboni slumbers and is dreaming. Sago ritual. Kanobo([2]), "the sacred cristal", wants a sago ritual. Again he sleeps and dreams. He fantasizes and sees the sacred cristal in his dreams.

3) *Tai hokona seribuya, Uboni. Dihana kanobo aru obonoya, nahanamu obonoya.*

At daybreak Uboni soliloquizes, informing the people. "The sacred cristal wants sago starch, he wants a nahanamu ritual.

4) *Yatu nokoyara? Nokoya. Nebu nokoya. Katukane yana.*

"Do you hear?" "Yes, we hear." The men are listening. "This way we are going to do it."

5) *Ine kanobo arima. Tane kware, ine yatu ahabara naute. Ine ahotana abate, ine nahanamu ahotana abate.*

I am the guardian([3]) of the sacred cristal. Therefore I will go ahead of you. I will start, I will start with the sago ritual.

---

[1] *Nahanamu*, literally, "the container of moriche stalks," the sago ritual, and for the commoner, a dance.

[2] *Kanobo*, literally, "our grandfather," the Supreme Spirit.

[3] *Arima*, literally, "the father."

6) *Yatu obononahakore inewitu abate, ayawarana manamo, ayawarana dihanamo. Ayawarana dihanamo abakore orabakaya, orabakaya.*

If you don't want to (chop sago), I will do it alone, perhaps two baskets full or three filled to the brim. Perhaps I manage three baskets or four, maybe four.

7) *Ine tara yakara ehobokore, ine diaranaka takore, hebu([4]) maminaka takore, ohidu masikabanaka takore, hima momu ahinaka takore, ine abate anamu orabakaya.*

If I remain strong, if I don't catch fever, if no disease-spirit looks at me, if no moriche palm falls on me, if I don't cut my foot with a hatchet, I will fill four baskets.

8) *Ayawarana orabakaya, ayawarana mohabasi. Mikore, tai ine konate, nahanamu abate. Uida([5]) abate, uida. Uida abate.*

Four baskets full or five baskets full. When I get them, I will bring them and launch a nahanamu ritual. Arrange a "large basket", a large basket. I will arrange a large basket.

9) *Tiarone, yatu mayamo naukore, yatu mayamo naukunaha tata, dihana oko nahanamu abate. Nahanamu ahokatane abate.*

Nevertheless, if you follow me, if you follow me there, we will arrange for a nahanamu dance. We will pour (the sago) into the container.

10) *Amaseke nebu dihana kokotuka ayamo bokoya. Ayamo bokoya, ayamo naruya.*

Right then all the men are getting ready. They get ready to follow the shaman, move behind him.

11) *Tata nabakaya. Uboni, oko hiamo naoae. Ah, yakara. Dihana nahanamu abakí.*

They arrive. "Uboni, we are coming with you." "Ah, very good. Let's set up the nahanamu container!"

---

[4] One meaning of *hebu* is spirit, another is ailment.

[5] *Uida*, a very large basket, but less than a *nahanamu* container.

12) *Nahanamu abaya. Tamaha abaya, ayawarana araisa. Ayawarana ariana, orabakaya, mohabasi.*

They set up the nahanamu container. This one and another basket full. They pour a third basket full and a forth, a fifth.

13) *Mohomatana hisaka, mohomatana manamo. Amasaba hisaka, mohomatana dihanamo.*

Six baskets, seven baskets. With this one, makes eight.

14) *Mohomatana orabakaya, amasaba hisaka muhinobo. Orikware tane mohoreko, mohoreko. Ayawarana mohoreko.*

Nine, and here another one, "the finger at the ed".([6]) All together ten, makes ten. Ten baskets to the brim.

15) *Tai konaya, tamatika nabakaya. Tamatika nabakakore dihana nahanamu namuya.([7])*

They bring the baskets and arrive here. When they arrive here, they already place the container.

16) *Tai nahanamu namuyakotai, mate tai nahanamuwituana.*

This is the "foundation" of the nahanamu container, but it still is not the real nahanamu ritual.

17) *Nahanamu namuyaha. Ahabara nahanamu namuyaha. Tatuka abaya, mate oriwakawituana, sanuka oriwakaya.*

They installed the nahanamu container. First comes the "foundation" of the container. They place it there, but this still is not the real celebration, they just dance a bit.

---

[6] *Muhinobo*, "the finger at the end," iqual to ten. The Warao system of counting is based on the number twenty, "*warao hisaka*."

[7] *Namuya*, this verbal term means to plant, to establish, but also stands for the preliminary ritual, *anamuna* as a noun.

18) *Nahanamu naha nonaya. Nahanamu naha nonaya, naha yewaraya, aru eku abaya.*

They prepare the moriche([8]) stalks of the container. They prepare the stalks of the container, finish positioning the stalks, and empty the sago in it.

19) *Aru sibia, eku abaya. Sibia, eku abaya. Sibia, eku abaya. Ebo hakotai sibia, moaya.*

They slice (a basket with) sago, and pour it into (the container). They slice it and pour it, slice it and pour it. What remains they divide and distribute (for the present meal).

20) *Kobenahoro moaya, kabitana([9]) moaya, bisikari moaya; moaya, moaya, moaya. Kokotuka daomatamo, kokotuka dihana.*

They give some to the (native) governor, some to the captain, some to the policeman; they divide, divide and divide. To all the grown-up men, they give to all.

21) *Ama nabakiemo erakate naoya, Aruabisi Akoho yatamo, Kohobaro yatamo. Tatukarao tamatikamo, era.*

Now some visitors also approach, those from Boca de Arawabisi, those from Kohobaro village. Those from here and there, many.

22) *Ama eku nahanamu, eku sanuka abanahakotai, dihana tai kate kokotuka oaya.*

Now those that only contributed a little bit to the container, all of them also took their part.

23) *Ine mayahotonae. Ine erakate borote, nahurute, ine erakate kwahana kabate. Matida namote.*

I was left out. "Me too I am going to chop sago, I will work the adze, I as well will fell sago-laden palms. My wife will knead sago pith."

---

[8] Moriche (*Mauritia flexuosa*), the Venezuelan (Carib derived) name for *ohidu*, the sago bearing palm.

[9] The office of kabitana is often said to have been instituted by the missions. It was, however, already in use by the time of Ralegh (1595).

24) *Yakara hemoate, makasea mataro eku. Araisa tuatane hese mataro eku. Araisa tuatane hese, tuatane hese, tuatane hese.*

"Alright, I will give you some in a calabash." The next one just the same in a calabash. The next one the same, the next one and the next.

25) *Atae nahanamu ekó, ekida. Tai seke nahanamu namuyaha, nahanamu.*

The container was empty again, nothing left. This really is the "foundation" of the container, of the nahanamu ritual.

26) *Mate ahabara nahanamu namuyaha, nahanamu namuyaha. Tai mate oriwakawituana, oriwaka ahotana abayaha.*

First you lay the groundwork for the container, the ritual's foundation. This is not the real celebration, it is the beginning of the festive cycle.

27) *Oriwaka nahanamu abayaha, oriwaka nahanamu abayaha. Tai ahabarakotai, maraisa.([10])*

This is the first thing you do, friend, when you organize a nahanamu ritual, when you arrange for a nahanamu dance.

28) *Sanuka oriwakaya, tamaha kanobo arima kanamunaya. Kanamuya, kanamuya, kanamuya.*

We dance a little bit, the guardian of the sacred cristal gets going. They all get up and going.

29) *Kanamuya wisatu([11]), wisatuhese, kabitana, kobenahoro, bisikari, daomata ine monuka.*

The wisiratu-shaman gets up and (then) another wisiratu, the captain, the (native) governor, the policeman, and the adult men like myself get going.

---

[10] *Maraisa*, "my other", my friend. While we were often called elder or younger brother, we generally stuck to the more forthright term "friend."

[11] Wisatu or *wisiratu* (in some areas *wisidatu*), a shaman that mediates between the people and the spirit world. The *kanobo arima* or guardian of the sacred cristal is always also a *wisiratu*.

30) *Kanamuya, yewará. Ama tahutuma dokotu awaratu kanamuya. Muhu atimuhitu kanamuya.*

They get up, finish (preparations). Now the old woman gets up who sings the sacred chants.([12]) The one gets up that clears peoples eyes by blowing on them.

31) *Ariatuka kanamuya, kanamuya, kanamuya, kanamuya, mohabasi, mohomatana dihanamo, mohoreko.*

A third one gets up, they all get up, five of them, eight, ten.

32) *Dihana yakara, mate yoriwakawituana. Oriwakaya sanuka, oriwakaya sanuka, yewará.*

That's it already, this is not the real fiesta yet. They celebrate a little, a little merrymaking, and finish.

33) *Tatukamo ubaya katukakore? Ama tamaha misa. Yaota hisaka([13]) eku ama seke dihana oko naute.*

How long will we wait [tarrying]? Today is sunday. On monday we will leave.

34) *Tamaha naruí taisia ha daukaba hakore mate ure([14]) namuya. Sikaro abaya, buratana abaya. Tai naruya misa kware du, yaota hisaka dihana.*

A rather large time-limit is given, so that people still can plant ocumo if they have a garden. They plant suger cane, they plant bananas. Sunday comes and goes by, it is already monday.

35) *Tai daukaba kokotuka dihana orinamuae. Sikaro namuae, buratana namuae, aru namuae. Dihana yaota aobonona hau tanaha.*

Already they planted everything in this garden. They planted sugarcane, they planted bananas, they planted manioc. Now they won't have to think about this work any more.

36) *Tai tatuka idate, aobonona isia idate tai. Dihana naruya kokotuka, nabakaya. Tuatane hese, maraisa. Tai emo nakanaha.*

---

[12] In this case the wife of Jaime Zapata, the "owner of the sacred clarinet."

[13] *Misa*, from Spanish mass, week or sunday. *Yaota hisaka*, literally "first workday."

[14] *Ure* (Colocasia esculenta), a loanword from Lokono Arawak, "ocumo chino".

Things will grow there, they will grow by themselves. (People) already leave and arrive (in the forest). Exactly like this, friend. We are keeping to the point.

37) *Kanahanamu tane borokí, nahurukí, kokotuka, oko ayawarana mite tai, mohoreko arai mohabasi. Yakara takore warao hisaka.*

Like this we chop sago for our fiesta, work the moriche adze, everything, until we have fifteen baskets full to the brim. When we have twenty it is all right.

38) *Warao hisaka mikore, yakara hese. Tai hebu nahoronaha, oko nahorote.*

When we get twenty (baskets) it is fine. These the ancestor spirit will not eat, we will eat them.

39) *Hebu saba nome abaya takore, tai hebu kanobo nahoronaha, oko seke anahoromo.*

Later we will prepare the ones for the ancestor spirit, these here the spirit of the sacred cristal will not eat, we ourselves are the fellow diners.

40) *Tai oko oriwakakitane, mate oko wabanahatihi, mate oko hatihi, mate oko sorobaetihi. Kahabaratuma moanobuae.*

So we will celebrate as long as we are alive, as long as we are here, as long as we are looking around. Our forbears they are gone.

41) *Tane tububuae, tane nahanamu ababuae. Ama tatuma moanae, oko anokeku mate ha. Tamaha nahanamu abayakotai, tai iabanaha, are hate.*

That's the way they made an effort, the way they organized the ritual. Now that they are gone, we are in their place. That nahanamu ritual they organized, we will not abandon, it always will be.

42) *Tuatane dibuya, kobenahoro dibuya, kanobo arima dibuya, wisatu araisa dibuya.*

That's how they are speaking, how the (native) governor speaks, how the guardian of the sacred cristal speaks, and the next shaman speaks.

43) *Kokotuka dibuya, maraisa. Boroya tata, mohabasi, ayawarana mohabasi, mohoreko.*

Everybody speaks, friend. They are chopping sago over there, five, ten baskets full.

44) *Atae mohabasi, mohoreko arai mohabasi. Amaseke tamaha kokotuka eku abate, nahoronaha.*

Five more, fifteen. Now they pour everything into (the container), but won't eat.

45) *Tai konaya, tamatika abaya. Tatuka abaya. Abakore, aru ayawarana kokotuka tatuka, atae naha yakeraha nonaya.*

They bring the sago and pour it here. There they pour it. When they poured all the baskets full of sago there, they prepare again good moriche stalks.

46) *Naha yakeraha nonae, hi, yewara. Ama seke eku abakitane. Hai, aukwa sanuka iabaya.*

They aprepare good moriche stalks, they finished. Now they pour everything into the container. They cut the top of the basket off and leave a little (for food).

47) *Ayawarana araisa haí, eku abaya. Aukwa sanuka uhu eku iabaya.*

They cut another basket open and pour its contents. A little rest they leave in the basket.

48) *Ayawarana ariana, haí.Tuatane hese orabakaya, mohabasi. Abaya, abaya.*

Another basket, they cut it open. In the same way four five more. They pour and pour.

49) *Dihana naha kwataya. Dihana naha tamaisia ha. Iakaya, iakaya.*

The container is already filling up, it's already up to here. They hem round the container with leaves (to hold back the sago).

50) *Idamo katamona? Idamo manamo. Idamo manamo mahanae. Tane mahaya, diboto noboto sanuka.*

How many grown men (with outstreched arms)? Two men (to measure the perimeter of the container). Two men join their outstreched arms, in front they add a small child.

51) *Tai nahanamu irida dihana. Aru abaya, nahanamu ha.*

It's a big container already. They pour sago, and the nahanamu (container) is ready.

52) *Ama aru sanuka aukwa kotai, aukwa sabasaba iabanahakotai, tai mokomoko orimoakitane.*

Now this little sago that was left from the top (of the basket), this leftover is distributed among (the people).

53) *Mokomoko orimoaya, tai mokomoko moaya, mokomoko moaya, mokomoko moaya.*

They distribute a little bit, give a little bit to him, to him and to others.

54) *Tamaha tai yaroko isia yehotobuya, dabo isia. Dabo isia hi hi hi. Hi. Tai tamaha sanamata.*

With a leaf they rub their hands (free of sago), or with a knife. Scraping with a knife, scraping. They scrape. This is really hard work.

55) *Tamaha sanamata, tamaha oko sanamatanae, tai yawanakomoni, tai yaroko aru hakotai.*

Tiresome, we had to put up with a lot, it should not fall (to the ground), the sago that sticks to the leaf.

56) *Horu hakore, horu eku abaya, tai yaroko aru hakotai. Ho isiko horeku abakore, tatuka dihana tai kokotuka ho aru hotakore.*

If there is a pot around, we put it inside the pot, the sago that sticks to the leaf. If you put it inside the pot with water, the sago dissolves with the water.

57) *Yaroko isia aru ekida. Tai horeku bahia ho isiko, tatukamo hi ya sanuka hi takore, yaroko haraha hakotai, aru ha, aru ha.*

There is no sago left in the leaf. It stays with water in the pot,and after a little while, the leaf is clean and there is sago, there is some sago.

58) *Tai sanamatatihi wayabutanaha. Yakeraha naoya, tairakate homo nahorokitane, homotane nahorokitane.*

Because we worked hard for it, we cannot throw it away. It comes out well and we eat it as porridge, in the form of porridge.

59) *Tane maraisa. Ama dihana yewarakotu dihana. Yatu dihana yatu sanamatanae, nahanamu kwatae.*

That's how it is, friend. Now we should finish up. "You did work hard, the container is full."

60) *Yewarakotu, yabakotu, yatu aobonona isia, yaotakotu aobonona isia. Yaotatu tiakore, yaotakotu.*

Finish up and go fishing as you see fit, work as you want. If you feel like working, do some work.

61) *Yaotatu tiakore yaotaya, yatu aobonona isia. Yaotakitane obonona-hakore, yatu aobonona isia. Aidamotuma dibuya, dihana nahanamu ha.*

If you feel like it, you work, just like you see fit. If you don't want to work, do as you wish. That's how the chiefs are talking, the nahanamu is ready.

62) *Tamaha anaya, ya hisaka. Tamaha ya araisa kanobo arima dibuya: Dihana ine hake, hake aniaukwa dihana ine namu yahakate.*

Night falls, one day (passcs by). The next day the guardian of the sacred cristal speaks out: "Early tomorrow morning I will enter the precincts of the sacred cristal."

63) *Namu yahakakore manokaba saba, okamutiemo, nehemanaka takore. Tata ine anate, yaha manamo, ya dihanamo.*

When I enter the precincts the fertile women should be waiting for me outside, so they wouldn't menstruate. There nightfall will find me for two or three days.

64) *Ine dara yahakate, daranamu yahakate, manokaba saba, yahakate, yahakate. Ya hakakore imana tai isia, tida hisaka naimakore, ya hisaka tata anaya.*

I will be inside closed doors([15]), inside the protected enclosure with you staying outside, and I will advance further. If time goes by and in the evening a woman has her period, she will stay one day´s nightfall (in the menstruation hut).

65) *Ya tai isia hese ehoboya. Ine hotu isiko kanobo aha moanaha. Tane ha, maraisa.*

That very day I will come out. With blood present I can't give tobacco to the ancestor cristal. That's the way it is, friend.

[15] No traditional Warao house or hut has really doors, but the upper part of the ritual hut is closed from view by temiche leafs.

66) *Nahanamu akabatu Uboni, tai Uboni hisaka. Anahurutu mauka Gerónimo, anahurutu araisa tai Eloy. Tai Uboni arawatuma, manamo.*

The moriche feller for the nahanamu is (the shaman) Uboni, only one man. Sago chopper is my son Gerónimo, another sago chopper is Eloy. These are the sons-in-law of Uboni, the two of them.

67) *Atae obonokore nebu daisa oaya, ariana tane. Tai Uboni anahurumo. Ama isimoi arotu Jaime (Zapata), tairakate tuatane hese.*

If they want to they grab another one, as a third (chopper). This is Uboni's team of choppers. Now, a team the same way is that of Jaime (Zapata), the owner of the sacred clarinet.

68) *Akabatu araisa Marco Zapata, warao manamo. Akabatu ariana tamaha daka nobarayahakotai, daka tai José Antonio wabayahakotai.*

Another moriche feller is Marco Zapata, this makes two people. A third moriche feller is this younger brother of mine, that younger brother José Antonio (Páez).([16])

69) *Akabamo dihana. Ama anahurumo: nahurutu ahabara mauka Brígido, nahurutu ahabara.*

So far the moriche fellers. Now the sago choppers: The first sago chopper is my son Brígido, the first chopper.

70) *Nahurutu ariatuka Francisco, ariatuka tai mauka aruwa, Dámaso. Ariatuka tamaha Esteban, orabakaya. Ama tamaha mohabasi, tai isimoi arotu auka, Ramón.*

Another chopper is Francisco, another my son's son-in-law, Dámaso. Another one that Esteban, makes four. Now the fifth is Ramón, the son of the owner of the sacred clarinet.

71) *Dihana mohabasi, nahurumo mohabasi. Tai dihana nahurumo.*

These are five already, five sago choppers. So far [those are] the sago choppers.

[16] José Antonio was ailing at the time (in the translation omitted).

72) *Ama namotu ahabara tai tamaha Jaime atida, dakoi sanuka. Oko waraya waraowitu doka.*

Now the first ranking at kneading (the sago mass) is Jaime's wife, my younger (classificatory) sister. In the Warao language proper we say doka.

73) *Tai namotu ahabara, dokotu awaratu, namotu ahabara, dokotu awaratu.*

This first person at kneading is the singer (of sacred songs), the first ranking at kneading is the singmaster.

74) *Ariatuka atekoro. Atekoro*([17]) *tai, dakoi sanuka atekoro, doka atekoro.*

A second person (at kneading) is her "helper", her co-wife, the assistant of my little sister, the co-wife of doka.

75) *Ariatuka marabai. Atuhe sabuka, mate iboma sabukakore. Ariatuka, tai mauka Brígido atida.*

A third one is my mother-in-law, long ago when she was still a fairly young woman. Another one is the wife of my son Brígido.

76) *Ariatuka tai Francisco atida. Namomo mohabasi, namomo.*

Another one is the wife of Francisco. They are five women at kneading, the ones that knead (the sago).

77) *Anamomowitu orabakaya. Anamotu dokotu awaratu isiko, mohabasi. Tane maraisa. Tane nahanamu borayaha, nahanamu nahuruyaha, nahanamu hakitane.*

There are four kneading women proper. Together with the singer, five. That's how it is, friend. That's how they produce sago for the nahanamu, how they chop sago, so that there can be a nahanamu (ritual).

78) *Nahanamu abayaha, tane. Isimoi arotu homakaba oanaha, nahanamu boroyakore. Tai isimoi arotu akabatu aidamo.*

That's how they organize the nahanamu. The "owner of the sacred clarinet" should not touch fish when they chop sago. This "owner of the sacred clarinet" is the chief of the palm fellers.

---

[17] *Tekoro*, "assistant" and co-wife of the principal wife, *hanoko arotu*.

79) *Ariatuka Marco Zapata, taikate homakaba oanaha. Ariatuka tai daka nobarayakotai, taikate homakaba oanaha.*

Another one is Marco Zapata, he will not touch fish either. Another (palm feller) is my ailing younger brother, he won't touch fish either.

80) *Taisia nebu idahidotumakotai, tatuma yabaya nahorokitane. Tiaha, tamatika tamaha kokotuka dihana, maraisa.*

Those younger men around, they fish for food. Now then, this is all, friend.

81) *Ama anamomo sabasaba, tamaha doka tai homakaba oanaha. Namotu ariatuka homakaba oanaha.*

Now, regarding the sago kneaders, that younger sister of mine, she will not touch fish either. The next kneader does not touch fish either.

82) *Namotu ariatuka homakaba oanaha, namotu ariatuka homakaba oanaha, namotu ariatuka homakaba oanaha. Tai kaunahuku oanaha.*

The next one either, the next one either, neither the next.
They should not smell the smoke of fish.

83) *Oko waruya waruowitu kaunahuku. Homakaba akona ahuku oanaha.*

In proper Warao we call it "the smoke of fish". They should not be exposed to the smoke of the fish brought here.

84) *Daisa, ibomamo daisa, tai homakaba oakitane, kaunahuku oakitane. Tai nahanamu ahokatane nahuruyatihi, nahanamu ahokatane namoyatihi.*

Others, other young women can touch the fish, be exposed to the smoke. Because the (former) chop sago for the container, knead sago for the container (they should not smell strongly).

85) *Tane maraisa. Tatukamo nahurutu ahabara mo obonaha, moho obonae tamaisia saka moho obonae, tamaisia naruya.*

That´s how it is, friend. Equally the first chopper should not open trunks for moriche larvae, wherever they open moriche for larvae he should make a detour. That's how they get on.

86) *Sibahia, dihana bahia. Dihana bahia, araisa dihana bahia. Nahurutu ahukatu tai moho oboya.*

They make a detour, they withdraw. They leave a distance, the next one leaves one as well. The last one of the choppers, he may dig larvae out.

87) *Nahurutu ahukatu tai hoku yabaya. Nahurutu ahukatu mukobo yabaya, kahu yabaya. Tai nahurutu ahukatu kware.*

The last one of the choppers, he fishes "guarapa" swamp fish. The last one of the choppers fishes mukobo catfish, fishes "guabina". Because he is the last one of the choppers.

88) *Nahurutu ahabara ehuru hakore, ehuru arotu. Ehuru ekidakore, musimoi arotu, musimoi arotu. Masi amuhu amaha mi batokonae.*

If there is a drum, the first chopper is the drummer. If there is no drum, he plays the deerbone flute, the deerbone flute. Look there, the deerbone flute that's hanging there.

89) *Masi amuhu, tai musimoi. Tai nahurutu ahabara. Ariatuka tane hese, ariatuka tane hese.*

From deerbone, that's where the deerbone flute is made from. (So behaves) the first of the choppers. The next one does the same, the next one the same.

90) *Nahurutu ahukatu isimoi hekunukabe, hekunukabe. Tai daukoho, daukoho awai. Awai tai hekunukabe.*

The last chopper plays the "yagrumo" flute, from the "yagrumo" reed. It is a wood with holes, it is called the wood with holes. Its name is yagrumo" flute.

91) *Hekunukabe ekoitaya muhusimoi akoita emo. Isimoi taikate hekunukabe emo.*

The sound of the "yagrumo" flute is different form the deerbone flute. The sacred clarinet also sounds different from the "yagrumo" flute.

92) *Tai naruya hokoya ha ahabara domu koitakore. Ahabara domu kou kou, tai dihana nahurutu ahabara kanamuya. Kanamuya aroko haraya, amu haraya.*

They leave at dawn with the first song of the birds. With the first bird song the first chopper gets up already. He gets up and washes his mouth, wishes his eyes.

93) *"Manebu! Dihana seisa! Nahurukitane!" Tai tata nabakaya nahurutu ahabara, kokotuka anebu mate tatuka ha.*

"Let's go, my fellows! Let's chop sago!" The principal chopper gets there while the men are still sitting around.

94) *Waha, nabawaha, nabawaha kabataya, kabataya, kabataya. Anebu hakotai hekunu yamakaya, hekunu kwai abaya.*

They cut dry moriche leaves, they cut and cut. The men ignite (the leaves) and hang the torches high up.

95) *Hekunu oaya tane. Tai nahurutu ahabaratihi dihana nahuruya.*

They thus grab the torches, because the principal chopper is chopping already.

96) *Oi, nahuru akoho narote. Tai kawahera, nahurutu ahabarakotai iboro kawahera. Ohidu kawaherakore kawahera tai, ohidu hunakawitu kabuka iabaya.*

Watch out that the adze does not hit the gunwale (of the moriche palm). It's long, the first chopper lifts a long strip of bark. A long piece of bark is lifted, at the very end a small piece of bark is left.

97) *Tai nahurutu ahabara saba. Ariatukakotai yahoto, autuabane. Ariatuka tuatane hese, ariatuka yahoto abane.*

This is the task of the principal chopper. The second one gets a smaller segment, in the middle. The next one the same, the next one gets less.

98) *Nahurutu ahukatukotai kabuka. Iyaka*([18]) *manamo, tai nahurutu ahukatu. Tane nahuruya.*

The last chopper gets a short piece.Two "leaves" long, the last chopper gets. That's how they chop.

[18] *Iyaka*, a measure, the length of a moriche leaf.

99) *Tai nahurutu ahabara nahuruya, nahuruya. Hukunu oaya. Anebu mate nahurutu ahabara nahuruyakore, tai awarao hakotai hekunu oaya.*

The principal chopper is chopping and chopping. They grab the torches. The men grab the torches when the first chopper is working, his relatives grab the torches (because it is still dark).

100) *Oaya, oaya, oaya. Hokoya ha dihana daunu nokanabú, daunu nokanabú.*

They light the torches all over the place. It is already dawning over the treetops.

101) *Dihana nahurutu ahabara samika iabaya. Tai samika iabaya hokonaetihi, hekunu obononaha.*

They leave the principal chopper alone by himself. They leave him alone as it is daylight already, he needs no torch now.

102) *Amaseke dihana nohibaya. Anebu hakotai amaseke iboro daisa nabakaya, hisaka hisaka borokitane, nahurukitane.*

They are pushing now. Those men now strip another moriche palm, to work each one on a different palm, to chop sago.

103) *Ine tamaha, ine tamaha, ine tamaha, ine tamaha. Ihi tamaha nahurutu ahukatu. Tane.*

This one is mine, this one is mine, is mine, is mine. You are getting that one, the last chopper. This way.

104) *Tai iboro nahurutu ahabara ekoroya ha, takore dihana ayamo.*

The piece of the principal chopper is finished already, and so (the women) follow him.

105) *Tamaha tai dakoi sanuka, doka, doka tamaha, dihana ayamo dokotu warakomo naoya.*

This little sister, the doka, comes after him singing here and there.

106) *Dokotu warakomo naoya, tai naoyakotai, dokotu waraya.*

She comes singing here and there, the one that comes singing.

107) *Tamaha manibora, manobotomo arima, masaba momonoko yakeraha abanae.*

"My husband, the father of my children, he prepared a good place for me to knead sago.

108) *Ekuya ine momu maka ine toaya. Maka orimatanako toaya.*

There I can move my foot and leg. It's a good place for my foot.

109) *Mawarao mayabatuma*([19])*, mawarao mayabatuma isiko. Manibora sisi yakera abanetihi. Tane dokotu warakomo naoya.*

Together with my relatives, contemporary women [agemates]. Because my husband prepared a good path (to walk on)." Like this she comes singing.

110) *Ebe saba aruwa, ebe saba abihi, tai isia kokotu waraya. Mebe saba maruwa, hikware ine naruya.*

There is the sago canoa, there is the sieve. That's what she is singing about. "Before me is my sago trough, I'm coming towards you.

111) *Mebe saba mabihi, hikware ine naruya. Dokotu awaratu tai, dakoi sanuka, doka, dokotu waraya nome, dokotu waraya.*

Before me is my sieve, I'm coming towards you." This singer, the little sister, the sister, she sings well, she sings.

112) *Ama ayamo atekoro araisa, ariatuka, araisa, araisa, araisa, ayaoyaba, tane wana awamo.*

Now comes the "assistant" (my second wife), and a third one, and another (woman), another and another, dance with me so that the bamboo flute will keep up.

113) *Wana awamo, wana ekoitamo, wana ekoitamo, tai are, arehese naruya. Aruwa kware nabakakore, arokohotu tuaraya.*

Those who keep the bamboo flute up, those who play the flute, This will always go on, always go on. When they get to the sago canoe, the singer will rest.

[19] *Yabatuma*, relatives of the same sex and age.

114) *Tuaraya. Kokotuka amaseke aruwa harakitane. Harahí, yewará. Watibuahi abakitane, watibuahi. No, watibuyana, watibuaka.*

She rests. All together they now clean the (inside of the) sago canoe. They wash it and finish up. They fix the conduit leaves. No, (I made a mistake), it's "the gutter to the sago trough."

115) *Watibuahi tai wahibaka abayakotai. Watebuaka, bihi awatebuaka.*

Watibuahi are the ribs (stretchers) of a dugout canoe. Watebuaka is the duct from the sieve (to the sago canoe).

116) *Kokotuka yewaranae, dihana seisa! Katukane dokotu warakomo?*

Everything is done, let's go! How are we going to sing?

117) *Aukwa hakore, arakobo sanuka hakore, arakobokore, tuatane dibu naruya.*

If there is a son or little brother, or a brother([20]), that's what they are singing:

118) *Hikware mauka, hiyehuna sanuka, hikware mauka, hiyehuna sanuka saba ine naruya.*

"For you my son, a little bit of new sago, for you my son, I am going for a little bit of new sago.

119) *Mebe saba orinaminanu! Mauka, arakobo sanukakore, dakobo sanuka, mayabatuma isiko yehuna sanuka saba.*

(Those sago choppers) before me, let's learn from each other! My son, or if it is a younger brother, little brother, going with my contemporaries [agemates] for a little new sago."

120) *Tai dokotu warakomo naruya, are hese, are hese, kware nabakaya.*

This singer leaves, stopping here and there to sing, always like this, always like this, and then she arrives (where the men are chopping sago).

---

[20] If a man or woman are speaking can be seen from the kinship term used, it is seldem directly expressed. Here, a woman is speaking.

121) *Kware nabakore, tamaha mi, ehunahakotai! Nahurutu ahabara ayehuna. Bomou dihana yewaranae, dihana yewaranae. Tane ha maraisa, tane ha.*

She arrives there, "look at this, the (amount of) sago that is there!" The new sago of the first chopper. A large quantity already finished,. already done. That's how it is, friend, that's how it is.

122) *Takore, anebu hakotai, ayabatuma hakotai, dihana uhu eku hokatubuya.*

Nevertheless, those workers, the women's age group, they are already filling the baskets (with sago).

123) *Autumowitu tai boto, ehuna, nahurunoko autumowitu moho isia nisaya.*

From the middle of the trunk they scoop the raw sago, the new sago, from the middle of the trunk with their hands.

124) *Moho isia nisaya, ayueku sai, araisa ayueku sai, ariana ayueku sai.*

They take (the sago) out with their hands and put it into a basket, another load into the basket, and a third load into the basket.

125) *Orabakaya, uhu autuya. Namotu ahabarakotai uhu autuya, namotu ahabara ayuautuya, bihi hisaka kayuka. Namokitane.*

There are four (women working), filling half a basket. The first kneader half a basket, filling a basket up to the middle, enough for one sieve to press out the sago (for the nahanamu).

126) *Ama ayabatuma tatuma seke dihana uhu ekwataya. Aukwa ihidoi, aukwa idoi, aukwa idoi. Tane.*

Now the group of young agemates are already filling the baskets. Filling up with a heap, up with a heap and up (to take home). That's how.

127) *Uhu ekwatubuya, tai seke namomotihi, anebu namomotihi.*

They fill the baskets because they are the sago kneaders, the workers who press (the sago).

128) *Namotu ahabara dokotu awaratu uautuya abaya. Yehuna abaya nahurutu yehuna uautuya.*

The principal kneader, the one that sings, puts half a basket. Half a basket of the raw sago that the choppers produced.

129) *Tai naoya tuatane hese. Tai bahiakotai naruya dokotu warakomo, naruya, naruya, naruya.*

They come that way and return singing a song here and there, they are leaving.

130) *Abihikware nabakakitane, nabakayaha. Dibuya: "Mabihi, hiekuwitu ine hinarote. Hiekuwitu ine hinarote mayabatuma isiko.*

They go towards the sieve, and when they arrive they sing: "My sieve, I will pour sago right into you. Right into you I pour together with my agemates.

131) *Mayabatuma isiko diatuka abihi eku mebesaba yatu kokotuka orinenibuae sakore, yatu ekuwitu oko hinarote. Hinarone oko kaobonona isia tate.*

With my agemates we will empty (our baskets) into the sieve which you already prepared before our eyes. We know how to do this without thinking."

132) *Dokotu waraya tai. Aributihi aruwakware nabakaya.*

That's how she sings. With these words they arrive at the sago canoe (with the sieves).

133) *Eku hinaroya. Hinaroya, hinaroya, hinaroya. Amaseke dihana namokitane.*

They pour the sago. They pour and pour. Now they start kneading.

134) *Tai dokotu awaratu bihi hisakatihi, namoya, baha iaraya. Oko Warao karibu.*

Since the singer only has one sieve full, she presses (the sago) and throws the sawdust away. That's how we Warao say it.

135) *Baha iarayakotai, wayabotaya. Tai yewarakore, tai namotu ahabara tai aututihi, bihi aututihi, tuaraya.*

The sawdust that is left, we throw it away. When this is done, the singer in the middle, since her sieve was in the middle, she rests.

136) *Mate anebu mate namoya. Uautuya bihi hisaka, uautana bihi araisa. Tane anebu hakotai.*

The (four) workers they are still pressing. Half a basket makes one sieve full, the other half of the basket makes another sieve. The workers do (two sieves).

137) *Ama dokotu awaratu hakotai, bihi hisaka uhu autuya konaetihi, tai dihana bihi hisaka namoya.*

Now the singer, she works only one sieve full as she only brought half a basket, she presses one sieve (of sago).

138) *Bihi hisaka namoya; baha iarakore, anebu wakaya. Tane maraisa.*

She works one sieve full; when she throws away the sawdust, she waits for her workers. That's how it is, friend.

139) *Ama, kotika anamomo hakore, kotika anamomo hakore, taikotai aboromo anahurumo saba, kotika anamomo.*

Now, if there are helpers with the kneading, other (women) that help with the kneading, those process (sago) for the men that do the chopping, the helpers.

140) *Tamaha, tai hebu aruwa, hebu aruwa, hebu aruwa. Tai eku aru hakotai, tai nahorokitaneyana.*

This here is the (sago) canoe for the sacred spirit, his canoe. The sago that is in there is not for eating.

141) *Tamasabaya tai kotika anamomo, taiseke anahurumo nahorokitane, tai isimoi arotu akabamo nahorokitane.*

Over there what the helpers process, that is for the choppers to eat, and for the palm fellers around the owner of the sacred clarinet.

142) *Tai tamaha hebu aruwa ahoka, aru hakotai, tai nahorokitaneyana. Tai hebu sabatihi, kokotuka abate.*

That content (sago) of the canoe belonging to the sacred spirit, the sago that is there, that cannot be eaten. Since it is for the sacred spirit, all is stored (in the nahanamu container).

143) *Tai namoya, tamatika ayaya. Tamatika ayakore, bihi yakeraha hoaraya.*

They press the sago, and here (around 2pm) they stop. When they stop working, they wash the sieves thoroughly.

144) *Hoarawihí, yewará. Watebuaka yakeraha hoaraya, wihí, yewará, yakeraha abaya.*

They wash them well, they finish. They wash the conduits [pipes] thoroughly, they wash, they finish, and then stow them away.

145) *Yakeraha abate! Bihi akoho ha. Bihi akoho ha, bihi akoho.*

"Stow them well! The sieves have a cord. The sieves have an 'ear', a string to hang them up.

146) *Tai ekuya oró, kwai batokoya. Kwai batokoya, kwai batokoya.*

With them you put (the sieves) in their place, you hang them up. You hang one up, and then the other."

147) *Dibuya dokotu awaratu: Yatu abihi kwai batokokotu! Dibuya: Yatu abihi namoru arai abanaka, namoru, namoru kwarisabamo abanaka!*

The singer says: "Suspend the sieves up (in a tree)!" She says: "Don't leave them on those rods, the sticks, don't leave them there on the tripods.

148) *Namoru kwarisabamo abanaka! Ama takatane kabihi yatu abihi bitahoro hakuna. Ibarinae sakuna.*

Don't leave them on the poles, so that they won't look like witchcraft, so they would not turn around.

149) *Tane kware namoru aukwata abanaka, bihi akohoko ha, kwai batokokotu.*

Therefore don't put them on the tripods, the sieves have hangers, hang them up."

150) *Namotu ahabara dokotu awaratu dibuyaha. Takore awarao ayabatuma dibu nokoya kwai batokonae.*

Thus spoke the pricipal kneader, the singer. Therefore the [relatives] agemates hear her words and hang the sieves up.

151) *Bihi akohoko hakore, ekuya abaya, ekuya abaya, ekuya abaya.*

As the sieves have an 'ear', they hang them up, all hang them up that way.

152) *Bató, bató, bató. Amaseke wiakitane.*

They hung them all up. Now to scoope the water from the canoe.

153) *Aruwa wiahí, wiahí. Nome aru wabae, aru wabae.*

They dry the sago canoe, scoope the water. There really is a lot of sago, a lot of sago.

154) *Ukabakeraha oko namoae. Nome okowituanatihi, kayuromo aobonona.*

The prove if the sago came out well, we sifted (the starch). It wasn't really ourselves but thanks to the spirit.

155) *Amasaba dibuya kayuromo aobonona kanamu aru wabae. Tamatika kanamunae satai Himabaka.*

People say that thanks to the spirit our container has a lot of sago. There the spirit Himabaka got going, "the one with the ax".

156) *Akabe esotanae satai, Himabaka. Kamiatanae satai.*

He has (the ax) hanging from his hip, (the spirit) Himabaka. He is watching us.

157) *Taisa obonona kanamu nome aru wabae. Himabaka aobonona.*

Through his doing, our container really has a lot of sago, thanks to the spirit Himabaka, "the one with the ax".

158) *Dihana anamuarao oriwakaya. Hi yewará. Tamatikamo nisakotu, tamasaba oanaka!*

Already the people who built the nahanamu container are celebrating. They finished up in a hurry. "Take from here (to eat), don't touch the sago over there!"

159) *Isimoi arotu naoya, nao dihana. Anoko ha dihana. Aru anoko abanaha dihana.*

The owner of the sacred clarinet is coming, he is coming already. The pla-ce (for the nahanamu) is prepared already, the place for the sago is set up.

160) *Ebukaria, ebuka araisa, ebuka ariana. Tahi isimoi arotu amoeku abaya.*

They take (a piece of starch) folding it. They take another and a third. They cut it and put it into the hands of the clarinet player.

161) *Konaruya, eku abaya. Tatukamo ebukaria, ebukaria, ebukaria.*

They bring (the piece of sago) and put it in place. Then (another woman) cuts a piece of sago. And so on.

162) *Aruwa tamaha ohidu hisaka, ohidu kawahera. Ohidu hisaka kawahera.*

This sago canoe is from one moriche palm, a very large moriche. One very large moriche palm.

163) *Kobowitu aru. Tane hese.*

Very full of sago. That very way

164) *Ebukaria, ebukaria, ariana tahi, dihanamo. Tahi abukaria, orabakaya. Tahi ebukari mohabasi.*

They cut a piece and then another and a third, three. Cutting a piece, four. Cutting another one, five.

165) *Tatukamo ebukaria, ebukaria. Tahi, mohomatana hisaka. owaraya, nowara isiko.*

From there they cut and cut. Cut, six. They arrange a communal banquet.

166) *Nabakanae mohoreko arai dihanamo. Dihana autu ebukaria, amukoho sabuka. Mohoreko arai dihanamo.*

They arrive at thirteen. They cut it in the middle and leave a rather large piece at the end, thirteen (pieces in all).

167) *Tatukamo tuatane hese. Mohoreko abukari abaya.*

From there on the same (by another woman). She puts ten pieces (unto the heap).

168) *Aru abakore ebukari mohoreko arai mohabasi arai dihanamo. Tatukamo atae abaya manamo, ebukari mohoreko, warao hisaka.*

They heap up cut pieces of sago, eighteen pieces in all. Then they add again two, cutting ten, twenty pieces.

169) *Mohoreko, mohoreko, warao hisaka*([21]). *Tamaha dihana ebukari mohoreko atae, warao hisaka nakayaha.*

Ten pieces and ten pieces, makes twenty. These are then ten additional pieces that complete twenty.

170) *Yakara dihana. Tamahakotai anahurumo saba, bonamu hisabakitane.*

So far so good (regarding the nahanamu container). The other lot is for the sago choppers, to cook a ball of sago.

171) *Tatukamo tahí, moaya namotu ariatuka. Tahí moaya ariatuka, tahí moaya ariatuka, tahí ariatuka.*

They cut and give to another (woman) kneader. They cut and give to another one, and another one, and another.

172) *Ama aruwa ahi amatana. Tahí moaya, tuatane hese. Tahí moaya.*

Now from the opposite end of the sago canoe. The same way they cut and apportion, cut and apportion.

173) *Dibuya dokotu awaratu, namotu ahabara dibuya: "Oi yatu bonamu iya hisabate. Bonamu hisabakotu yakeraha.*

Now the singer, the first kneader, speaks: "Watch out that the sago ball does not come out raw. Prepare the sago well done!

174) *Oi iya ehobote. Oko tomana ma tate. Tamaha yehuna mauka, arakobo sanuka hakore, ehuna yakeraha oko namoae.*

Careful that the sago does not come out raw. You will cause us disgrace. The starch produced by my son, and if there is a little brother, his sago, we did knead it well.

175) *Aru ukabakeraha namoae, boto, boto irida tubuyayana.*

We knead the sago throughly, the raw starch did not remain coarse.

176) *Boto mokomokera ha, namoae, tai kware yakeraha. Dibuya maraisa.*

The raw sago is finely kneaded, therefore it turns out well." That's what she says, friend.

---

[21] "One Warao," makes twenty.

177) *Ama namotu ahabara, dokotu awaratu, dibuya: Ine hisabate. Arakobo sanuka hakore, aukwa hakore, nahurutu ahabara saba.*

The principal kneader, the singer, says: "Now I am going to cook for the principal chopper," maybe it is a younger brother or a son.

178) *Bonamu sanukidayana, bonamu iridaha. Bonamu tamatika tai bonamu nahurutu ahabara.*

"Not a small lump of sago but a big one. It is for the principal chopper.

179) *Bonamu hisabaha, bonamu hisabaha. Tamaha ariatuka, mohabasi mohomatana hisakakore, manamo manamo.*

This ball of sago is cooked already, it is cooked." Here comes another one, five, six, handing out two by two.

180) *Manamo, manamo, manamo, manamo, ..namo, ..namo, tamaha nahurutu ahabara bonamu aidehemo manamo.*

Two, two, two and two. Two big lumps for the principal chopper.

181) *Tamatuma anebu saba. Hi yewará, hi yewará. Kokotuka tai tane moaya dihana, ayabatuma ahisaba, bonamu hisabakotai.*

The rest is for the workers. They finished up quickly, finished up. They hand everything out, those agemates that did the cooking.

182) *Dokotu awaratu kware toaya: "Tamaha dihana kahisaba." Taikotai uhu eku abaya.*

They hand everything to the singer: "This is what we cooked." They put the lumps of sago into the baskets.

183) *Uhu eku abaya hi autuya ehoboya. Bonamu witu, aru omi.*

When they did so the baskets were half full already. All lumps, no sago flour.

184) *Tamasabakotai awerea kotika namomo, tamatika hakotai hoyoya, namotu ahabarakotai moaya.*

The assistant kneader that is close rolls a ball (of sago) and gives it to the the principal kneader.

185) *Hoyoya, namotu ariatuka moaya. Hoyoya, namotu ariatuka moaya. Tai tata yarokore, namomo hakotai nahurumo saba imahakitane.*

Rolls a ball and gives it to another kneader, and so on. When they arrive (home), the kneaders make (sago) tortillas for the choppers.

186) *Tane maraisa.*

That's how it is, friend.

187) *Ya seisa, yewaranae dihana. Yaroko haria, uhu eku abaya, uhu eku abayatane dihana naria.*

They are leaving, they finished already. They gather leaves, put them into the baskets and leave.

188) *Amaseke isimoi koitaya. Tamatemo naruyaha isimoi koitaya, ama naoyarakate isimoi koitaya.*

Now they play the sacred clarinet. They go playing the clarinet, and from (home) they also come playing.

189) *Tai isimoi koitakomo naruya, naruya, naruya hanoko. Tai tamaha dokotu awarakomo aniaukwa naruhakotai, tuatanehese, maraisa. Tai ekuyahese waraya, maraisa.*

They go home playing the clarinet here and there. The one that left singing early in the morning does likewise. I am telling it really like it is, friend.

190) *Hanoko yaruyakore ebisaba aha, aha... tamaha mi, kaha.*([22])

When (the singer) arrives home she falls into the hammock... look, it's our bed.

191) *Maha mebisaba hoakanae sane. Ekuwitu ine, hiekuwitu ine, mahoi maka tuarate. Tai warakomo naoya hanoko yahakaya inaré tia.*

(She sings:) "My hammock hanging in front of me. In there, in you, my head and legs will rest." She comes singing and enters the house, quietly.

---

[22] Often formulated *ha ubakoina*.

192) *Ayu namuya. Ayu namukore, aributihi aheku tuaraya. Aheku tuaraya, aributihi aheku tuaraya.*

She sets the basket (full of sago) down. When she set it down, she rests in her hammock as she said. Resting in her hammock. As she said she rests in her hammock.

193) *Aheku tuaraya, aka ha ekuya ikahoya. Aributihi aka ituarayaha. Tane.*

She rests in her hammock, stretching her legs in her hammock. As she said, she makes her legs rest. This way.

194) *Tuarakore ama tai dibuya: Namomo mariatuka hakotai hekunu abakotu! Nahurumo saba aru imahakitane.*

When she rested she says: "My fellow kneaders, start the fire! Prepare the sago tortillas for the choppers.

195) *Tatuka inaré tanaka. Amaseke abaya, hekunu abaya. Abaya, abaya, abaya.*

Don't keep quiet." Right now they start the fire, They start (the fire) and kindle it.

196) *Aru saba abaya. Aru hisaba manamo, hisaba manamo, hisaba manamo, tane imahaya.*

They start to make sago tortillas, two tortillas (per person) each time, two tortillas. That's how they make them on the hearth.

197) *Aru saba kokotuka isimoi arotu kware toaya. Tamaha dihana karu saba.*

When they have the tortillas ready, they give them to the owner of the sacred clarinet. "These are our tortillas."

198) *Katamona ha? Aru saba tuatane ha. Mohoreko arai manamo. Aru saba manamo, manamo, manamo tane.*

"How many are there?" "This is how many there are. Twelve in all. There are two tortillas for each."

199) *Nahurumo mohabasi mahomatana hisakakore, manamo, manamo. Bonamurakate tuatane hese: manamo, manamo.*

If there are five or six choppers, two each. The same goes for lumps of sago, two each.

200) *Nahurutu ahabara arakate manamo, bihi manamo, iyaka manamo. Isana waranaha monuka, iyaka manamo. Tamaha aru hisabawitu iyaka hisaka, bonamu iyaka hisaka.*

For the first chopper there are two as well, on two trays, on two leaves. As I said before, two trays of leaves. For the sago tortillas a tray and for the lumps of sago another tray.

201) *Ama tai kanamuya, damitu isimoi arotu kanamuya. Tai mauka Brígido, nahurutu ahabara, kanamuya.*

Now my brother-in-law gets up. The "owner of the sacred clarinet" gets up. That son of mine, Brígido, gets up, the principal chopper.

202) *Ama tai damitu isimoi arotu kanamuya: Marawa! Tamaha dihana homo.*

Now the brother-in-law, owner of the sacred clarinet, gets up: "My son-in-law! The sago lump is ready."

203) *Yakara dihana marahi, sé, sé, sé. Bihi araisa. Ama seke aru saba witu.*

"Alright, my father-in-law." He carries it away. Now the other sieve, now to the proper tortillas.

204) *Marawa tamaha! Yakara marahi. Sé, sé, sé.*

"My son-in-law, take this!" "Alright, my father-in-law." He receives them elated.

205) *Abanae dihana. Bonamo bihi hisaka, aru bihi hisaka. Aukwaru ekida. Aukwaru ekidarone, nahorotekó ihisaha.*

They already put them down: the sago lumps on one tray, the tortillas on another one. There is no catch, meat or fish. Even if there is no catch, they eat (the sago) alone, hot.

206) *Ihísaha, nahorotekó. Dihana emo naruya.*

Quite hot they eat it, without anything else. They already go away.

207) *Damitu isimoi arotu dihana dokohotoya. Nahurutu ahabara, mauka Brígido, dokohotoya:*

The clarinetist, my brother-in-law, is already calling (the people). My son Brígido, the first chopper, calls (his men):

208) *Nahurumo, dihana makware naokotu! Makware naokotu dihana! Yatu mobukitine.*

"All you choppers, come here to me! Come here. I will hand out (the food)."

209) *Dihana nahurutu ariatuka, ariatuka, ariatuka: Homo manamo, aru hisaba manamo.*

The next chopper, the next and the next: Two lumps of sago and two tortillas.

210) *Homo manamo, aru hisaba manamo. Aru kayuka witu dú, wite orisaba aru hisaba manamo, homo manamo, nahurutu ahabara.*

Two lumps and two tortillas. The first chopper setting down two tortillas exactly, to each one two baked tortillas and two lumps of sago.

211) *Tane maraisa. Tamaha aukwa dihana. Tamatika witu tamaha aukwa, tamatika yewaraya.*

That's how it is, friend. This is the end already. Right here this is the end, here they finish.

212) *Tai boroyakotai are. Mate sinaria eku nakanahakore. Are.*

We will always extract sago. We will go on until (the baskets) are full. Always.

213) *Isana waranaha monuka, ayawarana mohoreko arai mohabasi mikore, aobonona nakakore, dihana tuaraya. Tane maraisa.*

As I said before, when we have fifteen big baskets full the way we planned it, then we will rest. That's how it is, friend.

214) *Hebu aruwa awere homakaba wahabunaha. Hebu aruwa awere moho obonaha.*

Close to the trough dedicated to the spirit, one does not roast fish. Close to the trough dedicated to the spirit, one does not dig out larvae.

215) *Hebu aruwa awere simo isobonaha. Hebu aruwa awere hoi kabanaha.*

Close to the trough dedicated to the spirit, one does not cut honey open. Close to the trough dedicated to the spirit, one does not slice "black bee" (pegón).([23])

---

23 Trigona sp.

216) *Tai hebu hoi ahuku ahakitane obononaha, tai hebu simo ahuku ahakitane obononaha, moho obonaha, ahuku ahakitane obononaha.*

This spirit does not want to smell "pegón," this spirit does not want to smell honey, this spirit does not want to smell larvae and the smoke (from roasting).

217) *Wahaburakate ahuku ahakitane obononaha. Tai nahorokitane aruwayana. Hebu saba tai aruwa, hebu aruwa. Waraya, hebu aruwa.*

Neither does he want to smell roasted (fish). No eating next to the sago canoa. This canoa belongs to the spirit, it is for the spirit. We call it the canoa of the spirit.

218) *Tai dibuya: Homakaba wahabukotu, ebure yatu kubate, wahabukotu tata.*

As the saying goes: Smoke fish, slay wild pig and roast it over there.

219) *Oi, tamasaba wahabute! Yehi sabasaba wahabukotu, akunahuku kemo hakakitane.*

Be careful not to roast over here! You have to do the smoking against the wind, so that the smell goes somewhere else.

220) *Tamasaba abane wahabukore ukunuhuku tamaha hebu aruwa yenite.*

If you roast (meat or fish) around here the smell gets to the canoa of that spirit.

221) *Tamatika tai aru ha. Kware nakate. Kware nakakore, kahunahuku tai aru kware tai yenikore, kanobotomo era, kanatoro era, oko sanamea takitane ha.*

Here is the sago starch. The (smell) gets to it. If it comes near, if the smell gets up to the sago starch, then many of our children, many grandchildren will suffer.

222) *Kanobotomo waba dibuidaha wabakitane ha. Waba dibuidaha wabakore kaobonona, kahunahuku tamasaba abanae.*

Our children all of a sudden get sick. If they get sick all of a sudden, it will be our fault, because we let the smell penetrate up to (the kanobo).

223) *Kahunahuku aru kware nakae. Tai kanobo yeninae, aru yeninae.*

Because the smell got near the sago. It penetrated up to the "sacred ancestor stone," up to the sago.

224) *Taisi aobonona tai oko wabae, oko onaya, oko takitane.*

Because of our fault we get sick, we weep, because we did it.

225) *Tanaka takitane. Yatu ebure mite, wahabukotu ahakayamo ahakayese saba saba, akunahuku kemo hakakitane.*

Don't do this. If you get a wild pig, roast it against the wind, so that the smell blows away.

226) *Tane maraisa.*

That's how it is, friend.

227) *Tuatakore, anamu ayawarana, kokotuka ayawarana, ayawarana witu, bihi, nahuru, isimoi kokotuka tata koyanoko eku tata deria.*

And when the container (of the ritual) is full, totally full, really full, all the (implements), the sieves, the adzes and the flute, all are taken to their place (in the ritual hut).

228) *Kanobo deria. Namotu ahabara dokotu awaratu dibuya: Nobo, nobo ya ine yewaraya, yawaranae dihana.*

They take it to where the "sacred ancestor stone" is. The first kneader, the singer, says: "Grandfather, I am finishing up already, grandfather, I finished.

229) *Tiatihi, seisa dihana. Tatuka ha hibihi, hinahuru, horurakate. Hiahoru, isimoi, kokotuka tatuka ha dihana.*

Therefore, let's go. There are your sieves, your adzes and also the cooking pan. Your cooking pan and clarinet, all is there already.

230) *Tai dihana hiabitu. Kokotuka deria, nahuru, bihi, isimoi, horu.*

It's all yours." They deposit everything, adzes, sieves, clarinet, frying pan.

231) *Dokotu awaratu kanobo ahanoko nohisaba nakaya, nahanamu atuka. Kanobo tata iakanaha.*

The singer arrives at the lower floor of the ritual hut, where the (sago) container is. She does not enter where the ancestor stone is.

232) *Hoaika nahanamu atuka seke nakaya. Tatuka nahanamu atuka bihi kokotuka abaya, horu abaya, nahuru abaya, isimoi abaya, kokotuka.*

Below where the ritual container is, there she arrives. There she lays down everything close to the container, the sieves, the pan, the adzes, the clarinet, everything.

233) *Ya tamaisia imananau, ubá, hokou. Dihana saba naruya, aru saba. Tata saba naruya, tata kawaheraha hakanaha.*

At about this time night fell, they slept and it dawned. They already left to where the sago was. That's where they went, they don't have to run far.

234) *Namokitane, amaseke karoko saba, oko nahorokitane. Tane maraisa.*

To knead (the sago) for our own mouths now, for us to eat. That's how it is, friend.

235) *Tai mate tanaka takore, emoarane mate dokotu awaratu tai namotu ahabaratihi mate derinaha. Mate kanobo yamonibuya.*

Since she is the first kneader, the singer has not deposited the sago (for the kanobo). The ancestor stone still has doubts (about the offer).

236) *Derikore seke tai musabera nakaya. Tane maraisa.*

When you hand over (the sago) (the kanobo) understands. That's how it is, friend.

237) *Tai Uboni... Isana waranae namomo saba saba.*

Now that (shaman) Uboni... Before I told you about the kneaders.

238) *Ama nahanamu yewarakore, nahanamu kwatakore, ama Uboni kanamuya, deria: Nobo, isana waranaha monuka, nobo, taisi dihana.*

Now, when the container is finished, when it is full, Uboni gets up and hands (the sago) over: "Grandfather," as I said before, "grandfather, here it is already.

239) *Hisaba abanae, taisi dihana. Tane kware, hiabonona isia tane.*

We prepared it for you, here it is. Therefore, do as you see fit.

240) *Oi, manohomona abate, oi, makoitabate, oi, ine onate.*

Watch out, you are going to freighten me, watch out, you will make me weep, watch out, I will cry.

241) *Manatoromo ha, domu hidotuma era. Oi nobo. Hiaobonona eku abanae, hisaba abanae.*

I have grandchildren, there are many new 'birds'.([24]) Watch out, grandfather. I did as you wished, we prepared (the sago) for you.

242) *Ihi obonoyatihi, hiaobononeku abanae. Tane nobo, taisi dihana.*

Because you wanted to, we prepared it according to your wish. Therefore, grandfather, it is done already.

243) *Hake, isana waranaha, tuatane aha himoate. Ama tai, derietihi, tai aniaukwa deria.*

Tomorrow," as I said before, "I will give you tobacco." In order to hand (the tobacco) over, the (shaman Uboni) brings it the next morning.

244) *Nobotomo arao, behorotuma arao hakotai, narubukotu tamaisia, taisia naukotu.*

(Uboni says:) "All the children, all dogs should bundle off, they should go away.

245) *Tamatika inaré obonoya, kanobo oriharakunarai inaré tane,*

I want calm here, so that the sacred ancestor stone may bathe himself peacefully,

246) *behoro akoita nokonaha sabuka, emoarane kanobo oriharayakore behoro ae ae ae ae ae,*

so he will not here the barking of the dogs, otherwise the dogs will squeal when the sacred ancestor stone is bathing himself."

---

[24] The "ancestor stone" looks on the people as 'birds' or pets.

247) *Takore tai kanobo yakeraha oriharanatate*[25] *asidaha. Asamatane oriharate, detana oriharate. Tane kware behoro arao kotai taisia arubukotu.*

Nevertheless, just when that sacred ancestor is taking the bath properly, it comes off badly. He can't clean himself well, he bathes with apprehension. Therefore all those dogs should go over there.

248) *Taisia ya dihanamo, waniku hisaka o waniku asibi, waniku asibi yatu ubate, tatamo nabakate.*

In about three days, or in one moon or half a moon... you will let half a month go by, and then you will come.

249) *Yakera dihana. Tai kanobo orihara yewaranae dihana. Uboni dibuyaha.*

It is done already. That ancestor stone has finished bathing already." Thus speaks (the shaman) Uboni.

250) *Takore ama behoro arao kotai taisia hoya bahia. Taisia naruya amasaba, tatuka inaré.*

All those dogs remain thereabouts towards the outside. They go over there; here all is quiet.

251) *Tai bahia kanobo arima, atida, aromutuma tai witu. Imananau takore, derihitihi dihana ubaya, Uboni ubaya.*

There remains the guardian of the sacred stone, his wife, and the pets. When night falls, he already sleeps as he has handed the offering over, Uboni sleeps.

252) *Ubaya. Ubakore amusotó. Oko Warao dibuya amusotó. Uboni amusotó. Dihana, tamaha ihi mamo hara?*

He sleeps. In his sleep he is dreaming. We Warao say 'he is dreaming'. Uboni is dreaming. Then, "is it ready what you are going to offer me?"

253) *Tamaha ihi mamoera? Tai ine hemoaha.*

"This is what you are going to give to me?" "This is what I am going to give to you.

---

[25] The "ancestor stone" takes a bath in the sago starch.

254) *Ihi oriharau! Ine oriharate, yakeraha oriharate, nokabaya ine aha bahate.*

Go and take a bath (in the sago starch)!" "I will take a bath, I will bathe carefully, and then I will smoke tobacco.

255) *Ine hahinate, nokabaya eku ine yahite.*

I will eat, and then I will lay down (in the sago container)."

256) *Uboni amusubuya saba warayaha. "Yakara." Amu dokó, tata naria dihana.*

That's what he told Uboni in his sleep. "It's alright." He wakes up and goes over (to the ritual hut).

257) *Uboni amu dokó, takore tata naruya. Kwai ahanoko ata naria. Darayata naria, kanobo ata.*

Uboni wakes up and goes over there. He goes to the ritual hut. He goes behind the walls (of temiche leaves), where the ancestor is.

258) *Naruya, naruya. Dihana hebu kanobo dibuya, aribu abaya, Uboni aroko isiko dibuya. Dibuyaha:*

He goes and goes. Then the spirit, the ancestor speaks, he makes a pronouncement, he speaks through the mouth of Uboni. He says:

259) *Ine hinobo. Ihi mamoae, nahanamu masaba abanae. Amaseke oriharae.*

"I am your ancestor. You made an offering, you organized a ritual for me. Then I took a bath."

260) *Yakera oriharau, moniana oriharau! Nobo, oi nobo! Moniana oriharau! Nokabaya manohomona oi.*

"Bathe yourself well, bathe yourself without problems! Grandfather, watch out grandfather! I don't want problems later (with people falling sick)."

261) *Uboni dibuyaha. Tai dibu nokonaha takore nokoya. Dibu nokoyayana, maraisa. Kanobo dibu nokoya.*

Thus speaks Uboni. (The ancestor) does not listen to anybody but Uboni. He does not listen (to others), friend. The ancestor listens (to Uboni).

262) *Tiaha tai imananau takore, tai kanobo aukwa isia, aukwa isia, aukwatana isia... nahanamu autuwitu naroya, naroyayama.*

And when night falls, the ancestor head first, head first... he plunges on end into the (sago) container, or so they say.

263) *Saín, nahanamu ote hoaika nakaya. Atae ehoboya, araisatane saín, atae ehoboya, ariatane saín.*

He falls into the container below. He appears again and a second time he plunges, he appears and again he plunges,

264) *nahanamu kwarisabamo, nahanamu aukwa yatuka. Diahanamo ehoboya.*

deep into the sago container, head first into the container. Three times he appears again.

265) *Saín, orabakaya. Orabakayatane aukwaya naroyayama.*([26]) *Orabakaya-tane aukwaya naroyayama. Taisike oriharayayama, maraisa.*

He plunges four times. Four times he plunges head first, they say. Four times he plunges head first, they say.([27]) That's how he bathes, friend.

266) *Oriharakore, orabakayatane aukwaya narokore, amaseke aha bahaya, aha.*

When he finishes bathing, after he went in four times head first, now he smokes tobacco, tobacco.

267) *Tamaha arokeku abaya. Tamaha araisa aroko eku abaya. Tamaha ariana aroko eku abaya. Tamaha orabakaya aroko eku abaya, dihana.*

He puts (the cigar) into his mouth, and the next one. The third one he puts into his mouth, and the fourth one. That's it.

---

[26] As the narrator is not a spirit guardian, he has not seen it himself but uses the "not an eyewitness" form.

[27] ′Four′ seems to be a key number, also regarding counterclockwise rounds on the dancing floor.

268) *Obono kobo, dihiana hahinae. Dihana, hahinayaha kayuka, kanobo hakotai aroko ekumo hehuku bomou.*

He has his stomach full and is satisfied. He is quite satisfied already, from the mouth of the ancestor stone comes a long strand of smoke.

269) *Ahikoto ekumo kahamanau, hahinanae. Dihana atae obononaha.*

From his nose come two strands of smoke, he is satisfied. He does not want more.

270) *Ahamara mohabasiyana, ahamara orabakaya.*

(He does) not want five wina cigars, four cigars (are enough).

271) *Tamaha moaya, tamaha moaya, ariana. Ahabara arokeku abaya, ariatuka arokeku abaya, ariatuka arokeku abaya. Tamaha orabakaya isia arokeku abaya, koyabaraya hiii autuya sabuka, ya bo saín.*

He gives him this (cigar), that one, and another one. He puts the first one into his mouth, puts another one into his mouth, an another one. When he puts the forth one into his mouth, he smokes and (the flame) goes up almost half the cigar, smoke comes out.

272) *Dihana kanobo hahinanae. Ahikoto ekumo hehuku ehoboyaha, kahamanau.*

Already the ancestor spirit is satisfied, From his nose smoke comes out in two strings.

273) *Ama nokaba tai seke ubaya, Uboni auba saba waraya.*

After this he sleeps, Uboni talks to him in his sleep.

274) *Ihi marima, ine hiauka. Ama eku yahite. Eku yahite, eku ine oribarabarite.*

"You are my guardian, I am your son. Now I will be in (the sago starch). I will be in it and turn around."

275) *Tai dihana, Uboni dibuyaha. Dihana oriharae. Aukwaya naronae, naronae orabakaya.*

"That's it already," says Uboni. He has bathed already. Four times he dived in head first.

276) *Tiaha aha moae orabakaya. Hahinanae dihana. Ama hakotai eku yahiteyama.*

The same way he gave him tobacco four times. He is satisfied already. Now he is in (the sago starch), apparently.

277) *Kanobo tamaha kahokonamu nahanamu eku yahiteyama. Tiatihi nobotomo sabasabaya kotubunaka takotu. Tamasabaya kotibukotu!*

That ancestor, our root, is reposing in the sago container, they say. "Therefore children, do not play around there. Go and play somewhere else!

278) *Oi, eku yahia. Amawitu kanobo nahanamu eku yahia, Uboni dibuyaha. Tane maraisa.*

Watch out, he is resting in there. Right now the ancestor is lying in the sago container," so says Uboni. That's how it is, friend.

279) *Bueno maraisa, ama oko warate. Oko abanae, kokotuka ha dihana.*

Well, friend, now we'll go on talking. We have taken notes of everything so far.

280) *Ama nahorokitane, nahanamu nahorokitane. Sinaria abaya, waniku akoyana tamahasia.*

Now the meal, consuming (the sago) of the container. The day of the feast is decided: When the new moon is at this height.

281) *Nahanamu kwatakore, tai waniku naruya, hí. Ayamo akoyana isia dihana yahobukitane. Yahobukitane, tai yahobuyakorehese.*

When the container is full, the moon passes by, passing. When the month is over, (people start) dancing a little. They dance a little, it's like a trial run.

282) *Tamaisia waniku honinakakore, dihana nahorokitane. Takore, tuatane takore, ama ubaya Uboni.*

When the moon is full, (the sago) will be eaten Now (the shaman) Uboni is sleeping.

283) *Uboni ubaya, musubuya. Uboni musubukore, dihana...*

Uboni is sleeping, dreaming. When Uboni dreams, already...

284) *Amusubuya aubaya waraya. Ihi marima... No, ihi dima. Dihana ine yawaranae.*

When he is dreaming in his sleep, (the ancestor stone) talks to him. "You are my guardian... No, you are the guardian. I finished already (bathing and smoking).

285) *Orihara yewaranae. Aha bahae, yewaranae.*

The bath is finished. I smoked tobacco and finished.

286) *Tiaha ama nahoro dihana, dihana nahoro. Nahoro . Nahorokitane ahabara ihi hohobute, hohobute, hohobute, hohobute, yakeraha.*

So, now the meal will start, the meal. Food. But before eating you will dance, dance a lot, dance well.

287) *Oi monikata. Dibuya, monikata omi.*

"Whatch out for quarrel." The ancestor stone says, "don't quarrel.

288) *Yakara hai enobukotu, kanobo dibuya, diboto Uboni dibuya. Dibuya katukakore? Katukakoreyana.*

Have a good laughter," says the ancestor stone, and Uboni answers. He says, "when?" "On that day.

289) *Hiabonona isia, hiabonona isia tanu. Dihana amaseke kanobo tai Uboni isiko dibunae. Dihana dibu yewaranae.*

It's up to you, whenever you like." Already the ancestor stone had spoken with Uboni. The conversation has finished already.

290) *Tai Uboni amu dokú. Kanobo dibuya, maisiko dibunae, maisiko. Ihi dima, satihi dihana yewaranae.*

That Uboni woke up. Said the ancestor stone: "You have been talking to me, to me. You are the guardian, therefore I already finished.

291) *Nahoro dihana! Hohobu nahoro! Tiaha ama aha atae ine bahakitane.*

Now go and eat. Dance and eat! Therefore I now will smoke again.

292) *Ine aha bahate, mabisikari aha bahate, makabitana bahate, matida hanokorotu bahate.*

I will smoke tobacco, the fiscal([28]) will smoke tobacco, the captain will smoke, my wife, the owner of the house, will smoke.

293) *Atekoro bahate, maromu behoroida bahate, kokotuka. Mamatana ha tata, tai bahate. Kokotuka aha moate.*

The second wife will smoke, my pet, the big dog, will smoke, verybody. The other one over there will smoke." Everybody is handed tobacco (to give smoke to the spirit).

294) *Oi hisaka yahotonae. Taisi nokabaya, amaseke mehokoituma. Mehokoituma kokotuka moakitane.*

"Watch out that nobody is missed (to receive tobacco)." Afer a while come the souls (the dead). "To all the dead you have to give (tobacco).

295) *Oi, hisaka yahotote. Hebu akohoko ekidarakate ha.*

Careful so that no (dead) one is missed. The ear of the spirit (defunct shamans) have nothing yet.

296) *Hebu kohokoana, hebu watayana, tatuma oi yahotonae, kokotuka moakitane. Kokotukawitu.*

The spirit 'without ears', the spirit 'without penis', watch out they are not missed, to all one must give, absolutely to all.

297) *Hisaka yahotokore, tai dihana kamu amoho abate. Tai dihana oko onate.*

If one is missed, he will already put his hand to our eyes (call you to die). That one will make us cry already.

298) *Hisaka yahotokore, tai dihana kamu abate, tai dihana oko onate.*

If one is missed, he will make us die, that one will make us cry.

---

[28] "Bisikari" (el Fiscal), the second in charge after the captain.

299) *Hisaka yahotonahakotai oriasite. Tai kamoho abate. Hisaka yahotonaka, kokotukawitu moakitane. Tane kanobo maisiko dibunae.*

The one that is missed will become angry. He puts his hand on us. “Don’t miss anybody, to everybody must be given.” Thus spoke the ancestor spirit to me.

300) *Satihi nebu, kabitana, kobenahoro, bisikari dihana nome abakotu. Dihana oriwaka, oriwaka.*

Therefore the men, the captain, the (indigenous) governor, the fiscal should now come together. The fiesta is on, the fiesta.

301) *Dihana orihara yewaranae. Musika imaya ine aha moate, aribu eku.*

They already finished bathing. “Later in the night I will distribute tobacco, as promised.”

302) *Tai kanobo arima nonae ahamara warao manamo, wina nonae ahamara warao manamo.*

That guardian of the ancestor stone had made forty cigars, he made forty wina([29]) cigars.

303) *Wisatu araisa mohoreko, wisatu ariana mohoreko arai mohabasi. Wisatu orabakayakore, mohoreko arai mohabasi.*

The next wisatu-shaman (has made) ten, the third shaman made fifteen. If there is a fourth wisatu shaman, he made fifteen.

304) *Tai ahamara yewará, dihana naruya tata darayata. Darayata naruya, tata kware nabakaya.*

He finishes the cigars, here he goes already to the ritual hut. He goes already to the ritual hut and arrives there.

305) *Kware nabakakitane... Asida... Tata narukitane yakeraha nakoya.*

To arrive there... No, wrong... Before going there he (the shaman) takes a thorough bath.

[29] Wina, the wrapping made from the dried husk of the winamoru palm (Euterpe spp., a variety of the “manaca” palm) into which rope tobacco is inserted.

306) *Tamaha kabesekuhu nisaya, hiaka hidowitu buaya. Hiaka hidowitu hau isia hidowitu abaya.*

He takes off his pair of pants, and dons a new loincloth. A very new cloth is fastened with a new string.

307) *Bua isiko naruya, tata kware nabakaya: nobo hi kware.*

He goes with his loincloth on, he arrives there (at the ritual hut), "grandfather, I came for you.

308) *Arai duhukitane. Hi korobakitane. Hi bisikarituma, hi kabitanatuma, hi nebu kokotuka korobakitane.*

To sit on (the wooden seat). To smoke with you. To smoke with your 'fiscales', with your captains, and with all your men.

309) *Ihi kokotuka hi isiko yewará. Nokabaya, hi matana.*

I finished up everything with you." After that comes the next one (the kanobo of Koboina village).

310) *Tai isiko yewará, maweriyemo wisatu araisa, araisa, araisa, ine dibunae, ihi mehokohi tai moau.*

Having finished with (the Koboina kanobo), the wisimo shamans were sitting (in a circle in the ritual hut), (Uboni) said: "You are going to give (tobacco) to that 'life force'.

311) *Ihi wisatu araisa, mehokohi tai moau. Oi, hisaka yahotonae. Kokotuka.*

Since you are one of the wisatu shamans, give to that ´life force´ (of a late shaman). Be careful not to miss one of them. All of them."

312) *Tiatihi wisimo awarao hakotai, tai mehokohi moaya.*

Therefore the round of shamans sitting there, were giving to the ´life forces´ of the defunct.

313) *Araisa moaya, araisa moaya, araisa moaya. Arima hoarotukore Hoebo sabasaba moaya.*

The next one is giving (tobacco), and the next one. One of the guardians who might also be a hoarotu shaman, give to the Hoebo spirit (in the West).

314) *Arima wisatu wabahakore, moaya. Ama, arahe arahe, arima arima dahu anonatu wahibaka anonatu wabahakore moaya.*

Another guardian gives to a defunct shaman. Now, if there is a difunct brother, a difunct guardian, a carpenter of hulls or dugouts, if he died he is given (tobacco by the living specialist).

315) *Tuatane.*

That's how it is.

316) *Ama tamasabasaba kware nabakaya. Tai moaya. Bisikari moaya, kabitana moaya.*

Now comes the turn of the rest. They are given (tobacco). The fiscal is given, the captain is given.

317) *Isana dibuya monukatane, atida hanokorotu moaya, aromu ehoroida moaya.*

As I said before, to the principal wife (tobacco) is given, as well as to the pet dog.

318) *Nokabaya mehokoituma kokotuka. Tai sabasaba, kokotuka,*

With time to all the defunct (tobacco) is given. It's for them, for all of them.

319) *tamaha hobahi arao hohosakotai hobahi isiko diawarabuaha, hobahi noisaba kanoika arao.*

It is for the ones that have been born in this land and were dancing, but now are under the ground.

320) *Ama tamaha nabeku, nabeku hayama oko kariawara.*

Now the ones that are in the rivers, the river-beings that are our origin, as the story goes.

321) *Oko monuka nabarao, kokotuka. Oko, tamaha kanoika saba hayama oko monuka. Warao.*

The river-beings are all like us. It is said they are like us, the ones that are down here. People.

322) *Tatarakate abayayama nahanamu. Oko tamatika hobahi arai nahanamu oko abaya.*

There they have a sago ritual as well, they say. Here on earth we organize a sago container (and ritual).

323) *Hohoyakotai tai monuka tata kanoi saba, kanobo hakotai saba nahanamu abakore oko monuka, hoho abayayama. Kokotuka.*

The same way we dance, down there likewise they arrange a sago ritual like us, and organize a dance, it is said. Everything.

324) *Ama dauarao, nokabaya dauarao. Dauarao, diharu arotu ha.*

Now to the beings of the trees, we come to the beings of the trees. The tree spirits, there is the "owner of the cedrillo tree."

325) *Tai daotubaka, diharu. Dauhorohi, dauhorohi. Oko waraya dauhorohi.*([30])

That cedrillo tree has its owner. The tree of monstrosity, the monster tree. We say the tree of disproportion.

326) *Tai nobotomo onayakore kayukau tia. Noboto onaya eh, eh, eh. Tatuka witu diharu ha, eh, eh, eh.*

If a child cries, the same way it is heard from the tree. A child cries eh, eh, eh. If right there a cedrillo tree stands, eh, eh, eh.

327) *Eh, kayukau tia. Sitaya dihana, noboto onayakotai tai sitaya.*

You hear eh. It is imitating the child already, imitating the child that is crying.

328) *Kasaba? Tamaha diharu tatuka. Ah, tai diharu arotu.*

Where? In that cedrillo tree over there. Ah, that is the "owner of the cedrillo."

329) *Tanahakore wasimoru, dau wasimoru. Tai arotu ha.*

If it's not this one, it's a "lechero," a rubber tree. It has an owner.

---

[30] Comment by Tirso Rivero: there are three trees one should not pass by with a child, *diharu* "cedrillo", *idu* "ceiba", and *dau wasimoru* "lechero" (a rubber tree).

330) *Tai isana waranae monuka, noboto onaya eh, eh, eh. Heh, kasaba? Tamatika, tamaha wasimoru.*

As I said before, when a child cries eh, eh, eh. Hey, where? Here, that is a "lechero" tree.

331) *Tai wasimoru tatuka aukwahata. Dihana sitaya.*

Up in the treetop of that "lechero" tree. It is already imitating (the child).

332) *Nomera? Nome. Tai wasimoru ahebu.*

"Is that true?" "It is true". It is the spirit of the 'lechero' tree.

333) *Ahebu. Tai hebu hebu botuka. Ama noboto onaya eh, eh eh, hobahi araiwitu onaya ha eh, eh eh.*

Its spirit. That spirit is a thin one. Now whenever a child cries eh, eh eh, right on shore there is a wail, eh, eh eh.

334) *Tai kanoisaba arao oko monuka aukwa bohí tanae. Aukwa bohí arani isiko. Aukwa bohí tanae amueku onaya.*

A head appears of the people down there that are like us. A head (of a child) appears with its mother. The (little) head that appears is weeping into the hands (of his mother).

335) *Tairakate hebu botuka hese. Tai nobarakore, tai sitaya nokone, diharukore diharu, wasimoru, hobahi araikore, hobahi arai.*

This too is a thin spirit. If the child gets sick when it hears that it is mimicked, when there is a cedrillo tree or a lechero ashore.

336) *Inabe namoyakore, tatamo hanoko yaroya, wisatu kware nabakaya. Wisatu waraya, wisitu saba waraya.*

If they are kneading sago in the forest, when they come home, they go for a wisidatu shaman. They tell the shaman, and speak to him.

337) *Ama maukatida onayaha kayuka sitaya, tamatika. Sina? Diharu.*

"Now my little girl is crying because up there it is imitated, here". "Who is that?" "The 'cedrillo' tree".

338) *Tuatane hakore wasimoru. Natukonu! Dihana wisatu imananau, wisatu dihana dokotibuya.*

Or maybe it is a 'lechero' tree. "Come and swing your rattle!" And in the night the shaman is singing already.

339) *Oko waraya dokohotu tihibuya, maraisa. Dokotibuya, dokotibuya. Dihana natokoya dihana.*

We here say 'to sing incantations', friend. He sings and sings. He is already working with his rattle.

340) *Nao ihira? Ine. Aha moaya. Aha moakore dihana inatabaya. Naru tamatikamo! Hi obononaha.*

"Come, who are you?" "It's me." And he gives (the spirit) tobacco. When he gave him tobacco, he already sends him away. "Go away from here! We don't want you."

341) *Tai noboto sitae. Tai wisatu waranaka takore, tai hebu naoya, ubayakore, oko Warao karibu, ahokaro([31]) nisaya, maraisa.*

This child was imitated. If they wouldn't call the shaman, that spirit would come in its sleep and, as we Warao say, take his heart, friend.

342) *Ahokaro nisakore, nobarakore, bahukanaha, wabaya.*

When he took his heart, when it got sick, (the child) will not recover and will die.

343) *Tane oko kasabsaba. Tane kware dibuya wisimo kokotuka.*

That's how it is with us here. That's why I told you all about the shamans.

344) *Dahu arao asida tubuyaha hobahi arao. Kokotuka aha moakitane, kokotuka.*

The tree spirits do a lot of harm to the people here on earth. We must give them tobacco, to all of them.

---

[31] Tirso Rivero points to his stomach, 'the heart'.

345) *Ama aha moa yewará. Diahana aisia dihana hohobuya, hohoya dihana.*

Now the tobacco giving is done. Over there they are already dancing, they already dance.

346) *Tata aha moaya dokotibuya, imautu taratu koyaukaya.*

Back there (the shamans) are offering tobacco and singing encantations, when at midnight a powerful (spirit) enters.

347) *Taratu. Waraya ine taratu, hi taratu, hi taratu, hi taratu. Ine taratu.*

A powerful one. Says he, "I am powerful, you are powerful, you are powerful, you are powerful (says he to each shaman). I am powerful."

348) *Tairakate hebu. Tairakate aha moaya.*

He is another spirit. He too is given tobacco.

349) *Aisia nebu daomatuma dihana hohoya. Hohoyakorehese hokou dihana.*

Over there the men and the elders are dancing already. Daybreak finds them dancing.

350) *Dihana kanobo arima ehoboya. Dihana uhu konakotu, yatu ayu konakotu.*

The guardian of the ancestor spirit appears (from the ritual hut). "Come and bring the baskets, bring the baskets to hand out the sago.

351) *Kabitana ayu, bisikari ayu, arisama ayu, daomatamo ayu, araisa ayu, kokotuka.*

The basket of the captain, the basket of the fiscal, the other one and the basket of the elders, the baskets of the rest, all of them.

352) *Oi aru asatate. Aru yawananaka oakitane.*

"Careful not to spill the sago. One should receive the sago without spoiling it.

353) *Tai sanamata, tai kayaota. Yawananaka yakeraha oakitane. Uhu autuya, autuya tane.*

It was arduous toil, it is our work. Take (the sago) without ruining it. Half a basket, half full to each.

354) *Oi yahotote. Manamo, dihanamo, orabakaya, mohabasi ahotokore, atae nahanamu borokitane takore tai yahotonahakotai, tai ama yatu sanetanaha.*

"Careful not to be short! If we lack two, three, four or five baskets, if we have to extract another container for what is missing, we won't help you (says Uboni).

355) *Tane kware, kokotuka oi yahotonae. Isana monukahese, araisa.*

Therefore all of you, be careful that no sago is missing." Just as I said before, friend.

356) *Kware abaya tamaha kobenahoro, tamaha kabitana, tamaha bisikari, tamaha daomata, tamaha daomata hese, tama' daomata hese, tamaha tai, tamaha tai, tamaha tai.*

So (Uboni) hands out (sago) to the (indigenous) governor, the captain, the fiscal, to this elder and to that elder, that much to him and that to the next.

357) *Ama tahutumakate tatuka ha. Mate sanuka nisakitine. No, isanaka!*

Now it's the turn of the older women. "I am going to get a little bit," (says one). "No, don't touch it!

358) *Mate aru iridawitu, mate yatu yawanakitia. Nokonaha tatuma hakotai.*

There is still a lot of sago left, you are going to spoil it." But those (women) are not listening.

359) *Inekate sanuka ine nisakitine. Ama sabamokate oaya.*

"Me too I am taking a little bit." Now they are taking some from the other side.

360) *Dihana naha hoaraya. Mate naha hoaranaka!*

Already they are pulling the stalks of the container out. "Don't dismantle the container!"

361) *Kawanuka, kawanuka arai namuya, tai naru amasaba nokonaha. Kwarika.*

Inside, inside the hut they come to blows with their hands, the ones on the other side do not listen. Harder still.

362) *Amasaba arahia nokonaha. Kwarika, manamo, ine namoae.*

Over there little sister dos not listen. Harder still, "it's my work, I have been kneading it."

363) *Aru tamaha ine namoae. Boroma eku nisaya, sinarianakaya, mataro eku, uhu eku, bebe yaroko eku nisaya.*

This sago I processed! They carried it away on a piece of tin, whatsoever, in a gourd, in a basket, in a plant leaf they take it away.

364) *Sanuka ihhh. Amayana aru yawanae. Kawanuka mate aru iridahasabukarone, aru asatae dihana.*

They heap it up a little. Done already, the sago is spoiled. Even if there was sufficient sago left (in the container), the sago was ruined.

365) *Tiarone ebo dihana aru ha dihana. Tamaha hiyu, tamaha hiyu, tamaha hiyu. Tata konaru! Konaruya, hohonoko arai abaya.*

Nevertheless, the sago is spilled. Here is your basket, here and here. Take it away! They take it away and pile it up on the dancing floor.

366) *Tamaha bisikari moaya, tamaha kabitana moaya, tamaha hiabitu, tamaha hiabitu, tamaha hiabitu. tamahiyu, tamahiyu, tamahiyu.*

They give a portion to the fiscal, and a portion to the captain, This is yours and this is yours. This is your basket, your basket and your basket!

367) *Tata konarukitane. Konaruya, hohonoko arai abaya. Tamaha moaya bisikari, tamaha moaya kabitana, tamaha hiabitu, tamaha hiabitu.*

It has to be taken away. They carry it and put it on the dancing floor, this is yours, this is yours.

368) *Tamahiyu, tamahiyu, tamahiyu.* (half a basket to each of the dignitaries). *Kokotuka kayuka? Kokotuka kayuka.*

This is your basket, your basket and yours. Is it well apportioned? Yes, it is well apportioned.([32])

---

[32] The distribution happens around 7am after a night of dancing.

369) *Sina yahotonae? Tai yahotonae. Konau, konau, anamu konau!. Ihikate boroae.*

Who is missing? This one didn't get any! Come on, come and bring a receptacle! You too were chopping sago.

370) *Ihikate boroae, ihikate nahuruae, hitida namoae. Ihi yahotokomoni, ihi yahotokomoni.*

You too were chopping sago, you too were pounding (sago), your wife was kneading sago dough. You can't go empty, you can't go empty.

371) *Anamu konaya, tamaha sanuka, tamaha sanuka. Tamasaba sanuka, tamá sanuka, tamá sanuka. Dihana ayu autuya nakaya.*

They bring a receptacle, this one a little and that one a little. Here a little, here a little and here a little. Already half a basket is filled.

372) *Oriwakaya. kokotuka yewaranae, yewaranae. Yakara dihana, yakara dihana.*

They are pleased. All is done, finished. It turned out well, well already.

373) *Kokotuka oriwakaya. Nahorokotu, inaretane! Oi tida habate, oi onate!*

All are celebrating. Go and eat, but quietly! Be careful not to hit your wife, don't make her cry!

374) *Kabitana, bisikari, kobenahoro, aidamotuma: oi aribu abate. Oriwaka tamaha, oko Warao oriwaka.*

The captain, the fiscal, the (indigenous) governor: Careful not to quarrel! This is a fiesta, we Warao are celebrating.

375) *Kahokonamutuma oriwaka, mate oko hatí, Tamaha oriwaka oko imoninaha.*

It is the fiesta of our ancestors, we still celebrate it, this fiesta will not be forgotten.

376) *Arehese naruya. Oriwaka abanae, yakeraha oriwakakitane.*

That's the way we always continue. We organize the fiesta in order to celebrate it well.

377) *Nakokotu, tuhutuma munawarakotu! Nebu akabamo aidamotuma nakokotu, yatu ahiaka daisa abakotu!*

“The women should bathe and paint their eyebrows. The elders who felled palms should bathe, and put on new clothing.

378) *Munawarakotu, barisa abakotu! Marana abakotu, tahutuma nasi dowaikotu, koko atoi habakotu!*

Paint yourself and use your painting pencils! Paint (your face) with drawings, the women should put on their necklaces, and grease their hair with coconut oil.

379) *Oi, dehe omi, monikata omi. Dibubu omi, oriwaka tamaha. Dihana oriwaka, dihana yakara, hobahi aidamo dibuyaha.*

Be careful, no slander! no quarrels! Don’t be talking too much, this is fiesta time. This is fiesta already, all is well”.

380) *Ama tiatihi tai aniaukwa, tai mate aniaukwa. Ya tamaisia kanamute, hokohi tamaisia.*

All this happens in the morning, it is still morning. When the sun is at this height people get going, with the sun up there.

381) *Era. Akabamo era, aidamotuma era. Kokotuka, hisaka hoho nakaeyana. Kokotuka hohote, kokotuka kanamute.*

Many people. Many palm fellers, many elders. All together, one alone can’t dance. All together dance, all get going.

382) *Tahutuma kokotuka kanamute. Hisaka hohonaha, kokotuka hohote. Hisaka hohonaka takore oriasite.*

The women all get up. One alone won’t dance, all dance. If somebody is not called to dance, she will get angry.

383) *Dihana naokotu! Sanuka nahoro yewará. Nakoya, hiaka daisa abaya.*

“Come on already! Get a bite to eat” They bathe and put new clothing on.

384) *Tida munawaraya. Tamaha amuwihi tamaha iwihia.*

The women paint themselves. They cut (and straighten) their eyebrows.

385) *Iwikoina isia hakore, muhiwihi isia hakore, isia wihia, wihia, wihia. Wihia, wihia, amatana wihia, wihia, wihia.*

If there is a rasor blade, if there is a cutting instrument, they cut their eyebrows and cut and cut. They cut here and there.

386) *Araya barisa abaya. Barisa amatana abaya. Tahutuma amunawarakotai tamaitane bomoutane.*

On top (of the eyebrows) they apply paint. On the other side they also (apply paint). The women paint long (eyebrows).

387) *Ou, amatana ou, awerea ou, awerea ou. Tai tahutuma amunawara.*

One stroke, here a line and next to it another line, (two lines on each cheek) That's how the women paint themselves.

388) *Ama nebu amunawara, amuwihi abaya, amatana abaya. Tamatikakotai abaya he amunoko, he amunoko mokomokoae.*

Now the men paint themselves, they paint one eyebrow and then on the other side (the eyebrow). They paint crabtracks, little dots as crabtracks .

389) *Tuatanahakore abaya, abuhene amunawara. Tuatanahakore abaya, abuhene amunawara atoritori isiko.*

If that's not the design they apply, they do the macaw motive. If they want another pattern, they apply little dots (over the eye), the blue and yellow macaw design.

390) *Barisa isiko. Tane. Abane, yiwará. Dihana munawarae.*

With a pencil, in such a way. They apply it and finish. They finished painting themselves.

391) *Ama daomata hisaka hisaka hakore, dihana oriwakakitane, dihana daunona ha, daunona ha, nonaya dihana.*

Now if there is one or the other mature man, they already start celebrating, the wooden daunona ([33]) figures are at hand, they are preparing them already.

---

[33] Wooden effigies of the *hebu* spirit in a male and a female version.

392) *Ihi daunona nonate, yakeraha nonau! Tida nibora, yakeraha nonau!*

"You are the one who is preparing the daunona figures, do them well! The female and the male, do them well!

393) *Hisaka kayuka, isimoi hakotai, hebu isimoi, dihana koitakotai tia.*

If there is an isimoi flute, a spirit flute([34]), one of the men plays (until the daunona is finished).

394) *Hebu isimoi waraya, 'aru simorokoni' waraya. Hebu isimoi waraya, koitaya.*

They play the spirit flute, they play 'one doesn't eat red (old) sago'. They play the spirit flute, it sings.

395) *Hebu isimoi koitaya 'aru simorokoni'. Hebu isimoi koitaya, hebu isimoi koitaya kaurubaka.*

The spirit flute sings 'one doesn't eat old sago'. The spirit flute sings and they sound the sewei([35]) rattle.

396) *Isimoi koitaya 'Wihi manamo', oriyahoro abane. Ama 'Wihi hisaka', isimoi koitaya 'Wihi hisaka'.*

The flute plays 'Two doves', (it is played by) two persons sitting together. Now they play 'One dove', the flute plays 'One dove'.

397) *Isimoi koitaya 'Hidani hisaka turatakitane'. Tai isimoi akoitahakotai are, tai daunona nonayakore.*

The flute plays 'Your mother got up alone'. That flute is always played, when the wooden spirit effigies are made.

398) *Daunona nonaya yewará. Ama noisabamo duhu ihidoya. Daunona noisabamo, daunona sá, sá, sá.*

The daunona figures are finished. Now a moriche leaf rib is sharpened (to hold the daunona). A little later they drive the (female) daunona (into the dancing floor).

---

[34] Technically, a clarinete.

[35] Carib loanword. The sewei (kewei) is used during fertility dances.

399) *Nibora tuatane hese. Noisabamo ihidoya sá, sá, sá. Sehoro wihia tamaisia abaya. Naha, tamasabaya naha, amatanaya.*

The male daunona the same. Next they sharpen the point and drive it into the ground. They peel the 'tirite' staff, they take 'moriche' palm slats and fasten them to the 'tirite' staffs.

400) *Nahawaha nasibine. Tamasia hau abaya, hau abaya. Tai nahawaha amunawara tida emo.*

They cut the moriche slats, and fasten them with moriche fiber, palm rope. The female slat is different from the male one.

401) *Daunona tida amunawara emo, nibora daunona amunawara emo. Ekuya hese.*

The female daunona you paint one way, and the male daunona you paint another way. One has to stick to it (see page 10, figure 6)

402) *Okoyone nibora oko nibo, oko Warao kamunawara emo, tida amunawarakate kemo.*

Even if we are men, if we are male, with us Warao we paint ourselves differently, the women paint themselves again differently.

403) *Tai monuka hese daunona amunawara. Daunona tida amunawara emo, daunona nibora amunawara emo.*

The same way you paint the daunona. The female daunona you paint one way, and the male daunona you paint another way.

404) *Nibora amubo abaya, tida amubo abaya. Tai yewarakore saín, tai hanokeku abanaha, hohonoko akari saín.*

They put onoto red on the male, and onoto red on the female. When they are done the daunona are driven into the ground, not where the (spirit) house is, but on the side of the dancing floor.

405) *Hohonoko akari atuka oró, awere oró. Kwarisabamo yasi hakore dú, hokohi oanaka takitane.*

You fasten one on the side of the dancing floor, and then you fasten the other one next to it. If there is a hat you cover it, so the sun will not hit it.

406) *Tane maraisa.*

That's how it is, friend.

407) *Daunona yewaranae. Amaseke kwarika koitaya, kaurubaka koitaya. 'Wihi manamo oriahoro' abane sitaya.*

The daunona figures are finished. They make a lot of noise with the sewei rattle. The (the shamans) imitate the song 'Two doves'.

408) *'Wihi hisaka' koitaya. 'Dani hisaka torá' koitaya, kokotuka koitaya.*

They play 'One dove'. Then they play 'Mother gets up alone', they play everything.

409) *Isimoi akoita hoitawitae, oriwakatihi, oriwaka.*

The flute plays on and on, because we are having the fiesta, oriwaka.

410) *Oko dibane 'bieta' takomoni. 'Bieta' tai hotarao aribu. Warao aribu oriwaka.*

We should not say 'fiesta'. 'Fiesta' is a criollo word. In Warao the (proper) word is oriwaka.

411) *Yakara, ama taisike oriwaka eku. Atida nehemate. Tai daomata atida nehemae dihana.*

Well, now we are in the middle of the fiesta. There is a woman who has her period. This man's wife has her period already.

412) *Tai nehemanoko eku ha. Sina atida? Taisi a tida. yakera dihana.*

She is inside the menstruation hut. Whose wife is it? That man's wife. It is alright.

413) *Tai oko dibukomoni. Eku kanamute. Nehemae anamotuaha, nehemae, tai anamotuaha nehemakore, anamotuaha nehemakore.*

We cannot speak about it. Inside these guiding rules they start (the dance). A kneading woman has her period, is menstruating, when one of the kneaders is menstruating, a kneader menstruates.

414) *Anamotu nehemae, anokeku daisa, tida daisa hohote. Tai eku abaya-ha. Mate. Aidamotuma era.*

When a kneader menstruates, another woman will dance in her place. Following these rules one proceeds.([36]) Wait a minute. There are many elders.

415) *Dihana dibuya, dihana, ya. Dihana hatabu namuya. Hohonoko autu saín, awerewitu saín.*

They are about to speak, already, now.([37]) They implant the arrow (of the daunona), they implant it in the middle of the dancing floor, and (the other daunona) next to it.

416) *Oró, oró. Autuya hau koyá. Nibora tamasaba sabasaba, tida tamasaba sabasaba.*

They drove it into the ground, into the ground. Then they tie them up with a moriche string. The male daunona in one direction, and the female in the other direction.

417) *Nibora hakotai takabe sabasaba. Tida hakotai kamotana([38]) sabasa-ba. Oi nobotomo! Nobotomo, himia, himia.*

The male is on the right, and the female on the left. Watch out children! Children, he sees you, he sees you.

418) *Hi nobo himia, nobotomo tatuka nakanaka. Tai daunona tai manamo oriwere ha, tatuka ha hebu.*

The ancestor spirit sees you, children should not come (to the dancing floor). Those two daunona figures are close, there are the spirits.

419) *Hebu tatuka ha 'Himabaka'. Tai daunona ayorotu. Ama oi nobotomo, ote naukotu.*

The spirit there is the 'Hatchet bearer'. He takes care of the daunona figu-res. Now watch out children, go far away.

---

[36] This woman is designated by the absent wife.
[37] From Spanish.
[38] *Kamotana*: for *kamoho amatana*.

420) *Ote naukotu! Dihana. Sina hebu sitate? Ihi Uboni, ihi yakera.*

Go far away! Now. Who is going to do the spirit? You Uboni, you are good at it.

421) *Araisa ihi. Ama tamaha Chano naruae hakotai. Dihana ebe yatamo Warao hisaka wabae, araisa Isaias wabae.*

The other one will be you. It will be this Chano([39]), the one that just left. Time ago one man died. The next one, Isaias, he died (as well).

422) *Tatuma hebu asitamoyaha. Tai isiko hisakatane dihana, maraisa, hisakahese.*

Those that used to portray the spirit (had died). They are already one with that (spirit), friend, they are together.

423) *Uboni, ihi Chano, yatu hebu sitakitane. Dihana. Namuyata narute, Namuata. Tai namu, kwaihanoko manamo, dara dihanamo.*

Uboni and you, Chano, you will portray the hebu spirit. Already done. They leave for the spirit hut, for the sago container. That container, the spirit hut has two (floors) and three walls.

424) *Kwaihanoko namu dara dihanamo. Tata mataro manamo ha. Kasabukaha konate?*

The spirit hut (with the nahanamu) container has three walls. There are two (sacred) rattles. Which one (of the calabashes) will they bring?

425) *Arose hakotai taiwitu konau! Tai kanobo isiko akobemaha, akobemaha, kanobo akobemaha,*

Bring the one with plumes!([40]) The one that is next to the ancestor spirit, tied to its stomach, nexto to the kanobo spirit,

426) *kanobo isiko aubatu, akobe amahatu, tai konau! Araisa konau!*

the one that lies next to the ancestor spirit, that is tied to its stomach (heart), bring that one! Bring the other one too!

---

[39] A son-in-law of the narrator. During the recording he had left on a trip.
[40] *Arose* means literally club, but in shamanic language it means feathers.

427) *Tatamo ehoboyaha, tai darakoho tane emuraya. Amasaba koyaya, amasaba koyaya.*

(The shamans) appear from there, they open the door from there. They tie (the screen) here and tie it there.

428) *Tai dihana duhunoko tamaha, toatiaha duhunoko diaka ha. Tai tatamo hohoyaha mikitane, miaha.*

That is the coffer (used as a shaman's) seat, it is now in full view. (The spirit) observes from there how they dance, it observes them.

429) *Mikitane, mikitane, monikata ekida, monikata ha. Tatuka ibomamo nehematu ahotu isiko hohoyaha miaha.*

In order to observe, if there is a quarrel or not. It watches that no girl with blood from her period is dancing.

430) *Tai kanobo darakoho emuranae, oko waraya darakoho emuranae, tai kanobo sorokitane.*

That ancestor stone (is watching) through the open door, we say 'the door is open', the ancestor stone is watching,

431) *Tida sina seke nehematu hotu isiko tai daunona awere hohoyaha, hohote. Hohoyaha.*

What woman with blood from her period is dancing next to the daunona figures. She is dancing.

432) *Takore hebu aobonona emo ehoboya. Tuatane maraisa, darakoho emuruya dihana, emurá.*

Nevertheless, this is not what the ancestor spirit wants. That's how it is, friend, the door is already opening, it opened.

433) *Amasaba koyá, amasaba koyá. Tatamo naoya dihana. Araisa amoheku abaya, mataro araisa araisama amoheku abaya.*

They tie (the palm curtain) on both sides. Here the (shamans) are coming (from the ceremonial hut). They put the remaining rattle into the hands of one of them.

434) *Dihana hebu sitakitane! Turá, araisa awere turá. Dihana nokanahobuae.*

Let's start acting the spirit! (One wisatu) places himself, and the other one stands next to him. (The two) are already standing there.

435) *Tai dihana daunona aukwa miatubuae. Uriabane kawaraya, kawará, ayamo kawará.*

They are already gazing at the head of the daunona figure. They take a slow step, a pace, and behind him the other makes a pace.

436) *Hebu, hebu sabaekitane! Hebu isia dibukitane! Sina? Daomatamo.*

Go and insult the spirit! Talk to the spirit! Who should? Some grownups should.

437) *Ihi yakera, ihi yakera. Orabakaya. Kawará, kawará, kawará.*

You are good at this, and you are good. The four of you. They take a step, a step and another step.

438) *Hisaka, tatukamo atae aka nisate. Araisa, tatukamo atae aka nisate.*

One round, and from there another round. The next one, and another round.

439) *Ariana sibahite, ariana. Ihi miae, maraisa.*

Another round, and a third one. You have seen it, friend.

440) *Tatukamo atae nisate. Orabakaya, tai dihana. Tatuka nakakore dihana mataro ekoitaya, saí, saí, saí.*

From there they make another round. Four rounds, that's it. When they arrive (at the starting point), they make the rattle sound, saí, saí, saí.

441) *Aho, hebu hawanera tane, hebu hawanera tane. Hebu bosi hakore, hebu tamaha bosi era.*

Ah, this spirit is dangerous, a dangerous spirit that one. Let's see if the spirit has a wound, that spirit has a lot of wounds.

442) *Hebu amuhusi, hebu amuhusi noborobuae. Mm. Hebu kwana nohibaya mohoro.*

The footnail of the spirit, its nail is split in two. Mm. Perhaps the spirit is working hard.

443) *Hebu kwana nohibaya mohoro. Hebu hobahi kwana yabukaria mohoro. Tai kware tamaha hebu hokwaruta, enoya. Ihi miae.*

Perhaps the spirit is making an effort. Perhaps the spirit is stamping the ground. Therefore this spirit is lecherous, it is laughing. You saw it.

444) *Tane ha. Tane dibuya. Tane dibuya, atae araisa tane. Tuatane hese. Isana waranae monuka hese, maraisa.*

That's how it is. (People) are talking like this. They are talking like this, and the next one is doing likewise. Really like this. As I said before, like this, friend.

445) *Saí, saí, saí, ahh, hebu. Ariana, tamatika dihana isimoi arout ha. Isimoi arotu kanamuya.*

Sound the rattle, ah, the spirit. Another one, there is the 'owner of the sacred flute' already. The 'owner of the sacred flute' is getting up.

446) *Tahutumarakate dihana tai nome abane ha, orinome abanaha dihana, wiribukitane, hohokitane.*

The grown women too are already prepared, they help each other getting ready to leap about and dance.

447) *Wiribukitane, hohokitane, dihana orinome abanae. Yewaranae.*

To do the nahanamu leap and dance, they prepare each other (for the dance). So they finished up.

448) *Ariana, orabakaya, amaseke nohibakitane! Dihana sibahikitane.*

A third, a fourth (round), now make an effort! Already turn around.

449) *Sibayakore dihana isimoi akoita nohibakitane. Sibayakore dihana isimoi akoita koitakitane: De, de, de...*

When they turn around([41]), the sound of the flute is energetic. When they turn around, the tune of the sacred flute is sounding: De, de, de...

---

[41] The movement is counter-clockwise.

450) *Amaseke hohokitane! Ahabara hohoya, hiae. Araisa, hiae, ariana, hiae. Tamaha hiae orabakaya.*

Now to dance! First they dance, then they shout. A second dance, another shout; a fourth dance, a shout. They shout four times.

451) *Mohabasi nakanaha, moho matana nakanaha. Orabakaya, hiae, hiae, hiae. Hiae orabakaya.*

They won't shout five times, won't shout six times either. Four times, they shout and shout. They shout four times.

452) *Ama sina? Sina takomoni, ihi! Kanobo arima. Kanobo arima dibukonaha kobenahoro.*

Now, who (will dance)? It will be you, the guardian of the sacred ancestor stone! The guardian shaman suggests the (indigenous) governor.

453) *Kobenahoro, kobenahoro, kobenahoro! Kobenahoro, ihi sina ha? Tane. Kanobo arima dibunae: Ihi ahabara hohoteyama.*

Governor, governor, governor! Governor, where are you? That's it. The guardian shaman says: "It seems you will be the first to dance."

454) *Tane kware kobenahoro kau. Tane hese, maraisa. Hohoya, araisa, ariana, orabakaya.*

Therefore the governor is getting up. Just like this, friend. They dance, another, a third and a fourth.

455) *Nibora hisaka ayamo tahutuma orabakaya hohoya. Ihi naminaya. Taisi ariatuka kobenahoro ariatuka amaseke kanobo arima hohoya.*

Before one man there will be dancing four women. You know (how it is done). After the (indigenous) governor the spirit guardian will now dance.

456) *Tai hoho yewarakore, amasaba ha wisatu. Tai wisatu hese, tatukamo kabitana, ama tatukamo daomata.*

When the (spirit guardian) finishes his dance, a shaman (will dance). After the shaman comes the captain, and then an adult man.

457) *Daomata hese, bisikari, daomata hese. Ihhh...! tai kokotuka daomatamo. Besó.*

Another adult man, the fiscal, and another adult man. Ihhh...! all the older men. Finished (the adult men).

458) *Nahurutu ahabara, maraisa. Ihi miae. Sina nahurutu ahabara? Ihi!*

(Then comes the) first chopper, friend. You have seen it. Who is the first chopper? You!

459) *Brígido nahurutu ahabara. Nahurutu ariatuka, ariatuka, ariatuka, ...atuka, ...atuka, ..atuka.*

Brígido is the first chopper. The next chopper and the next, another one and another one.

460) *Besou. Tatukamo amaseke asinaria omi. Kokotuka hohoyakotai mohabasi hohonaha. Sibahia, sibahia, sibahia, sibahia, tahi imoninaha.*

The choppers finished. Now they continue without counting. Those who danced will not dance five rounds (but only four).([42]) One round, and another round, four in all, they should not get confused.

461) *Anowarutu ha, tamaha ariana. Tamaha awahabara. Kwana dibuya, tamaha awahabara. Oi, kwarea wayabate.*

There is always somebody counting, "this is the third (round). This is the first one. He says in a loud voice, "this is the first round. Be careful not to do another round!

462) *Oi, yahotorakate ha! Kwana dibuya.*

Watch out, you danced one round too many!" He speaks energetically.

463) *Tai kokotuka besou. Amaseke dihana tahutuma. Tida mahaya, tahutuma hohokitane.*

That (part) was all finished. Now it's the turn of the women. The women line up, the women will dance.

---

[42] Four is the sacred number among the Warao.

464) *Sina ahabara? Dokotu awaratu, tai ahabara. Tai mutemoikitanetihi, mutemoikitane.*

Who will be the first? The singleader is the first. Because she is the one that blows over the eyes (of the four young men), blows over the eyes (to cure them).

465) *Mutemoikitanetihi, tai yakera ahabara, dokotu awaratu. Ihi awahabara!*

Because she cures their eyes, she should be the first, the singleader. "You are the first!"

466) *Tatuka ha arowai nasi kawahera. Tamaisia batokoya, ihi miae. Nasi tehere kanobo arima koyaya.*

She (*wears) a very long necklace of beads. There is one hanging (pointing to one hanging on the wall), you saw it worn. The spirit guardian attaches the tehere bell.*

467) *Atae sanuka bahikí. Nasitehere kanobo arima koyaya, wisatu koyaya.*

Let's regress a little. The spirit guardian fastens the tehere bell, the wisiratu-shaman put's it on.

468) *Kobenahoro koyaya, bisikari koyaya. Wisatu hese, daomata hese, daomata hese, daomatamo.*

The (indigenous) governor fastens it, and then the "fiscal". Likewise the wisiratu-shaman, and then one elder, another elder, the elders.

469) *Nebu nahurutu ahabara hisaka koyaya. Ariatuka koyanaha.*

Among the commoners only the first chopper puts it on. Nobody else puts (the tehere bell) on.

470) *Tatukamo nasi tehere koyanaha. Taisi monuka, maraisa.*

From then on they do not wear the nasi tehere, the ritual bell. Like this (the ritual goes), friend.

471) *Tai dokotu awaratu, tai mutemoikitanetihi, tai kanamute, hohokitane. Ihi miae, maraisa.*

That singleader, because of her blowing over the eyes, she will get up to dance (first). You have seen it, friend.

472) *Ine dibuya: Miarone([43]) dakoi sanuka! Miarone, miarone, miarone! Mariboto dibuya: se dakobo, se, se, se!*

I tell her: "Come to dance, little sister! Come and dance!" She answers: "Well, brother, here we go!"

473) *Daunona akau nabakaya. Taikate tuatane hese, maraisa. Nasi tehere koyaya.*

She arrives to where the daunona are, (the wooden spirit effigies). The (women alternate) the same way (as the men), friend. They put on the nasi tehere bell (tying it to their necklaces).

474) *Nebu daisa daisa tane. Nebu iabaya, ihi ama. Ihi ariana.*

(Four) men dance one by one. One man (dances a round and) leaves. "It's your turn! You are the third one!"

475) *Tai ayasi abaturakate daisa ha. Tamaha nasi tehere abatukate daisa ha. Nasi tehere daisa abatu, ayasi abatu daisa.*

The one that wears the ritual hat also changes. The one that holds the ritual bell changes as well (They are standing without dancing). Another one holds the ritual bell, another one wears the ritual hat.

476) *Tai barikore hoho ayewará, hoho ayewarana barikore, yasi dao, hiaka eku du.*

When they finish taking turns and the dance ends, when they dance the final turn, they take the ceremonial hat off and put the (red) cloth into it.

477) *Hiaka abatukotai, nasi tehere abatu hahia. Ama tida kawaraya.*

The one that wears the cloth, the next one with the ritual bell loosens it. Now the woman turns around.

478) *Tida dibuya, tida dibuyakotai, huliane, huliane dakobó! Huliane, huliane, huliane.([44]) Ine diboto dibuya: se, dakoi sanuka, se, se, se.*

The woman speaks, she says: "I already danced jumping, brother! I danced leaping, danced, danced." And I answer:"well, little sister, well done."

[43] Come to dance! (in shamanic language).
[44] Shamanic language for "I danced leaping."

479) *Tamaha erokonaka, maraisa. Emo nakanaha, daisa ekida. Ariatuka tuatane hese, ariatuka tuatane hese, ariatuka tuatane hese.*

This is unmistakable, friend (only the old ones use it). It is done properly, there is no other way. The next one does the same, and the next one as well.

480) *Ibomamo oakore, nasi tehere dihana batokonaha. Ibomamorone daomatamo mate aukamotamo erawituana hakotai. Erakotai, anoboto erakotai, tai nasi tehere isiko hohoya.*

When it is the girls turn, the ritual bell is not worn. This applies even to young women with few children. The ones that have many children dance with the ritual bell.

481) *Mate anobotomo manamo, dihanamo, orabakaya, nasi tehere isiko hohonaha. Tai tuatane tai soroya mate, tai tatamo mia.*

The one that has only two, three or four children, does not dance with the nasi tehere bell. That (kanobo stone) is still watching, it watches from afar.

482) *Ama tai tatukamo tahutuma ibomamo nasi tehere omi hohoya. Kokotuka besou. Dihana yewaranae. Tahutuma isana waranae...*

Now, from there on the young women dance without the tehere bell. Everything is finished, it is already over. Now the women, as I said before...

483) *Tamaha daomata atida nehematu. Oko tai hohonatatera, hohokitane ha. Dibuya, anaka ahabara.*

There is an elder whose wife has her period. We (are discussing) if he can dance, if he should dance. But he says, he first has to go (to his wife in the menstruation hut).

484) *Anaka ahabara atida nehematu aobonona nokokotu. Ya ayabatuma hakae. Hi nibora ikanamukitane obonoya.*

"Go first and listen what the menstruating woman has to say." Already some of her agemates hasten there. "Your husband wants to go (and dance)."

485) *Ihi oriasina([45]) hara? Ama hinokekurakate hohote? Hinokeku. Ihi nehemae, anamotuyaha.*

Are you going to get angry? Now, who is going to dance in your place? In your place. You are having your period, you the one that has been kneading (sago).

486) *Ihi anamotuyaha nehemae. Katukane monuka ha? Atida katukane dibuya?*

You have been kneading (sago) and now you have your period. What will be going to happen? What will the wife say?

487) *Hohokunarai tanae! Hohokunarai tanae! Oriasina hara? Oriasinaha.*

"He can dance! (says the wife), He can dance!" "Won't you be angry?" "No, I won't be angry."

488) *Hohokunarai tanae! Enobuyaha, enobuyaha. Enobuyaha, ha ha ha. Oriasina hatai. Aidamotuma yorohatí, daisa yoronaha.*

"He can dance!" She is laughing and laughing. She is laughing, ha, ha, ha. "I won't be angry. The elders will take care of him, nobody else should interfere."

489) *Aidamotuma. Aidamotuma bisikarituma, kabitanatuma. Ikanamuyatihi yakara. Hohokunarai. Ya hohoya. Hohí, yewará.*

The elders. Elders like the "fiscales" and the captains. (The man) gets up and dances alright. He goes to dance. He is dancing already. He finished dancing.

490) *Nehematu anokeku kanamukitane. Nehematu anokeku. Nehematu anokeku kanamute. Kasabukaha kanamute?*

Somebody has to get up in place of the impeded wife, in place of the prevented wife. Somebody will get up in her place. Who is going to get up (and dance)?

---

[45] For *oriasinaha*.

491) *Ihi yakara, ihi mate hohonatanae. Ama hinokeku kanamukitane obonoya. Kasabukaha yakara?*

You are alright, you haven't danced yet (the women say). (One woman) is willing to get up in your place. Which one is alright?

492) *Tai manokeku kanamukunarai! Tai arahia hakore, dahia manokeku kanamukunarai. Ine nehemae, manokeku hohokunarai tai.*

"That one should get up (and dance) in my place! (says the wife) That younger sister, my little sister should dance in my place. As I am prevented, that one should dance in my place."

493) *Tatamo dehe isiko naoya, dahia manokeku kanamukunarai, hohokunarai tanae. Arahiayama, daisatuma obononaha.*

From (the menstruation hut) comes the news, "the younger sister should get up in my place and dance." The younger sister, it seems; no other should interfere.

494) *Ah, yakara. Arahia ha. Tai. Araiba nehemae, anokeku hohokitane ha.*

It is alright already, there is a little sister. It is her. Her older sister has her period, and she should dance in her place.

495) *Tai seke atida nehemá, aobonona nokonaka, nibora hohokore, atida nakokore, anibora isiko orisabahikitane.*

If a wife has her period and her husband doesn't listen to her wishes and dances anyway, he will have problems with her after she (comes out and) bathes.

496) A*nibora kanamane atida yewerekitane. Monikata hakitane. Tane maraisa. Monikata ekida takitane, saba warate yakara.*

The husband that danced then will beat his wife. There will be a dispute, friend. So that there should be no quarrel, they should properly consult.

497) *Hohokitane! Araisa yakara, hohokitane. Asida dibate, no, hohonaka takunarai. Oi, hohote.*

Off to dance! If a friend is agreed upon, off to dance. If (the wife) says no, (the husband) cannot dance. Woe is he who dances.

498) *Ine nehemae, ine nehemae. Taiyama sibahia taiyone yakara, taiyone hohoya dihana. Tane kware kanamunaka, hohonaka takunarai.*

I am having my period, I am barred (from dancing). Even if he wants to take turns with the others, alright, if he would be dancing already. Therefore he should not get up, should not dance.

499) *Tane dibunaerone hohokore, dihana orisabahikitane, oriyewerebukitane, orisiki asidaha dibukitane.*

If he dances in spite of everything, they are already quarreling, already hitting each other, and are interchanging swearwords.

500) *Tane ha. Tamaha oko kahokonamu, oriwaka nahanamu. Eku, tane ha. Ama yewaranae dihana, hoho yewaranae.*

That's how it is. These are our roots, the sago festival. This is the setting, that's it. Now it is over already, the dance is over.

501) *Ama tatukamo mate yewaranaha, ahukatu sanuka ha. Sina namotu ahukatu wayabate?*

After this not all is over, there is a little tail left. Who of the sago kneaders will close the dance?

502) *Ihi, Hiyosimo! Hiyosimo, ihi wayabate! Ihi dihana anaminatu! Isana waranae tuatane hese, maraisa.*

"You, Hiyosimo (name of a woman)! Hiyosimo, you will close the dance! You are an expert!" Exactly as I said before, friend.

503) *Tamaha isia dihana wayabaya. Wayabakore tai Hiyosimokotai ahara kwai abanaka tatuka nohibaya. Daunona tatukaya nohibaya.*

Therewith they close the dance. Closing the dance that Hiyosimo jumps without raising her arms.([46]) She will jump around close to the Daunona staffs.

---

[46] The women closing the dance will jump around with their arms risen and attack the men jokingly.

504) *Tatuka noakaya, noakaya, noakaya. Diá, hiae! Tamaha yewarayakore, ama ebure.*

After that she turns around jumping. Done already, and hej! (the people shouting). When this is over, now (they imitate) the wild pig.([47])

505) *Ebure kasabamo? Tamasabamo! Tamasabamo kahe ebika, tamaha kahe ebika.*

From what direction do the wild pigs come? From over there!
Over there (they were seen) the day before yesterday, they were seen.

506) *Tamasabamo! Tai hiae takotu. Tamasabamo kahe! Ama tamasabamo, ahia sabasabamo.*

Over there! (They point) so that people will shout. Over there yesterday! Now over to the other side, upriver over there!

507) *Ahabara yariboto sabasabamo! Kahe ebika! Nabaida sabasabamo kahe!*

First (they appeared) where the sun rises! The day before yesterday!([48]) Yesterday (they were seen) towards the coast!

508) *Omunoko kahe. Ahia sabasabamo ama anakwarika, ama anakwarika.*

Yesterday (they saw) the footprints! Now in the afternoon (they saw them) somewhere upriver, in the afternoon!

509) *Yaroko kwai toaya. Yaroko kwai toaya, ebure hae! Ebureyama, tamasabamo kahe ebika.*

(The people) are heaping up leaves. "They heap up leaves," (shout the people), "there are wild pigs! Wild pigs, it seems, over there the day before yesterday."([49])

510) *Tamasabamo kahe. Tamasabamo ama anakwarika, ama nakwarika ebure ha.*

Around there yesterday. Around there now in the evening, now in the evening there are wild pigs.

---

[47] Dissimilar to the "old world" pig, called in Venezuela 'váquiro'.

[48] There are two groups among the crowd: the people and the wild pigs.

[49] Shouts between the two groups of people.

511) *Tai ebure mate tatuka yewaraya, yewará, kwarima sabukau, dose nikabataya.*

Those wild pig (people) there finish (talking), they finished and then waited a little, they cut sticks (to beat the pigs).

512) *Kabataya, kabataya, kabataya. Dihana ebure... Ihi ahabara, ihi ebure aidamo! Habi sanuka amoeku du. Tane orikahoya.*

They cut and cut (sticks). The wild pigs already... "You are first, you will lead the pigs!" They put the little rattles in his hands (to lead) and fall in line.

513) *Tamaha karamunaya, hü, hü, hü. Ai, ai tiakotai auka, noweteyaha, aukawe. Araisa sibahia eku hese, maraisa, hoho eku hese.*

They cause a commotion, wä, wä, wä. Their little ones make ai, ai, the bunch is hungry. They turn around, friend, according to the dance.

514) *Ariana sibahia. Tamaha moteomo sibahiakotai dihana kasibahia. Hi warakotu.*

They do another round. The ones that have danced four([50]) rounds, they already leave. They should shout "heee!"

515) *Oi, oi, moanubuahayama, ahotukatidu aru hisabayaha ahoru, ahoru hinaroneyama, maraisa.*

Watch out! ([51]) According to our ancestors, a goddaughter (of a wild pig) was cooking a large vessel, and it seems somebody turned the vessel over.

516) *Tububuaha, mate ine ekidakore. Tai hiahotukatida ahoru... Ahisaba oi hinarote.*

This happened when I was not born yet. Your goddaughter's vessel...Watch out, the cooking (of your goddaughter) is falling over!

517) *Katukane? Nokonaha eburetihi, eburetihi. Dau isia tosinae aru isiko hinaronae.*

How come? They don't listen because they are pigs, are pigs. With a stick they turn (the pot) and knock it over with the sago.

---

[50] Literally, the fourth finger.

[51] A story is blended in here.

518) *Ah, ebure tai katukane, tai hihotukatida ahoru, tai ahotukatida ahoru, katukane aru hisaba hinaronae?*

Ah, how did those wild pigs (turn the cooking sago over), the vessle of your godchild, that godchild's vessel. how did they turn the cooking sago over?

519) *Ebure nokabasaba sabahia. Tai nokonaha, tai dihana hü, hü, hü. Taihese naruya, taihese naruya, taihese naruya, taihese naruya.*

They shout insults after the pigs. They don't hear, they already (make) hü, hü, hü. One (pig) passes by and then another one and another.

520) *Hanoko sibahia, kanobo ahanokoata nakaya. Kanobo ahanokoata nakaya. Tata Warao asibia ha.*

They do a round of the (spirit) hut, and arrive there. The (wild pigs) arrive at the spirit hut. (The people) half of the Warao are (waiting) there.

521) *Mate, mate kwarika eku nakakotu, kwarika! Eh, dihana hisaka ahatatu ha. Hisaka dokohotoya.*

Wait, wait, the pigs should fill the (ground floor) of the spirit hut. Hey, there is an archer already (to shoot the pigs). One is shouting (to scare the pigs).

522) *Ah, ebure nabukaribukotu. Hih, dau, dau, dau, dau. Damana hakaya.*

Ah, so the pigs should disperse (to all sides). Hey, he caught one, caught another and another (pig). A few escape.

523) *Tai ote ha, hohonoko sabasaba. Tata Warao hakorekate, dau. Tida hakorekate oaya, dau.*

There is (a pig) far away next to the dancing platform. But there are some people as well to catch them. A woman is there as well, she catches (the wild pig) and stops it.

524) *Dihana tatamo ebure konaya. Tamatika aró mahaya. Aró mahane konaya, tamaha tuatiaha oane konaya.*

Already they are bringing the (dead) pigs from over there. They carry them on their backs. On their backs they carry them and in that fashion they bring them.([52])

525) *Kokotuka konaru. Tai ebure konae yewará hohonoko arai nakaya. Hohonoko arai nakakore tamaha dau mokomokokotai, nobotomo tamaha tuatiaha mokomokeraha hakore, bueno, arima nisaya.*

They bring all of them. They bring the (dead) pigs and let them fall on the dancing floor. After they fall on the dancing floor, they throw away the [little] sticks.([53]) If there are [many] small children, well, their father takes the stick (to throw it away).

526) *Hi hiahara wakera, tehoto nakate. Tamaha ebure aukwa arose tehoto nakakore, asida. Ihi idamotanaha ihi wabate.*

"Your arm is weak, (your throw) falls short (of the ritual hut)." If the stick to hit the pigs on their head falls short, it's bad. "You will die without getting old."

527) *Nakakitane kanobo ahanoko kwarea. Kwana, kwana toakitane! Mate tatukamoana, kawarakotu!*

It should fall beyond the spirit hut. "Further, throw it further! Not from here, step further ahead!

528) *Ote, aweremo! Tehoto nakanaha, kanobo ahanoko tehoto nakanaha. Tai yatu aukwa arose nakakitane!*

Further away, from closer to the hut! (That way) it will not fall short, not short of the spirit hut. That's where the stick (to hit the pigs) on the head should fall!

---

[52] From the ritual hut wich is located in the forest some 200 meters to the east.
[53] The sticks "the people" held in their hands to hit the pigs.

529) *Ebure hanoko kwarea, digo*([54]) *kanobo ahanoko kwarea. Naruya, naruya, naruya, naruya, awere sabuka, kwana toaya.*

Beyond the house of the pigs, I mean, beyond the spirit hut." They step further and further, coming rather close and throw with force.

530) *Oi, dara kanobo ahanoko isia nakate, kwarea. Tai ebure aukwa arose toayakore, ayamo soronaha. Dibuhida toaya, toaya, toaya. Tane ha, maraisa.*

"Watch out it doesn't fall next to the door of the spirit hut, further!" When one throws the stick, one should not watch it (fly).([55]) They throw it quickly, one after the other. That's how it is, friend.

531) *Tai tatamo tai yewarakore, amaseke dihana. Amaseke dihana ihi dibuyamonuka tane hatabu. Ebure tamaisia, ebure tane baria, Warao hakotai tamasabaya.*

When they finish, [right now already] (all return to the village). This is the part of the arrow about which you asked before. The "wild pigs" are over there (to the side), they move that way, the "people" (move) the other way.

532) *Tane maraisa, tai kanobo naminaya dihana, orinaminae. Ihi, ihi kanobo arima, ihi ahabara dihana! Yakeraha abaya, yakeraha abaya, orimahaya. Mate dibunaka.*

That's how it is, friend. The ancestor spirit knows already, they tell each other. "You are the first spirit guardian!" (The people) should post themselves properly (in two lines) and take their arms. They should not talk yet.

533) *Orimahaya bomou. Amatanaya orimahate bomou. Kaurune naria dihana. Kaurune tei, tei.*

They take their arms and form a long line. The others also form a long line They walk stamping their feet. They stamp their feet tei, tei.

534) *Até bahia. Araisa, ariana, orabakaya. Ekuhese, maraisa. Tai tamatika, tai tamatika nakanaha, ekuyahese.*

Again they return.([56]) Another round and a third and a forth. (Four) exactly, friend. They won't make a mistake, (it is four rounds) exactly.

---

[54] The narrator reverses himself in Spanish.

[55] Only the shamans watch how it flies.

[56] Only men, the "people" and the "pigs."

535) *Amaseke 'ohosese'. Ooosé, ooosé, oosé, oosé, ehhh!*

Now comes the shout (of throwing the arrow): Osé ehhh!

536) *Araisatane: Oooosei, osei, osei, ehhh. Dihana orabakaya hese.*

The next (turn)... (sound of rising arrow). The fourth (turn) is done already.

537) *Oi, mate oremo sabuka. Mate oboribu kwasikore.*

Careful not to stand too close. They won't leave enough room for the shaman.

538) *Ama hatabu! Oko dibuya kwahasika, tai kwahasika tatuka.*

Now the arrow! As we say: high up, it should go up as high as possible.

539) *Kwahasika eburunu, kwana! Kwana hatanu! Bomou.*

Toss it high up in the air, vigorously! Shoot the arrow forcefully! Far away.

540) *Eratihi, nebu eratihi yakara takore. Nebu eratihi dau. Tai hohetanae dihana. Yatu amoho ekoitakotu Pai Paiyó.*

Since there are many men, they should catch it alright, (it should not fall to the ground). As there are many men, one caught it. He is the lucky one. You have to whistle with your fingers ("Pai Paiyó.")

541) *Tai hohetanae dihana. Mate ama araisa. Tuatane hese, maraisa. Ihi miae.*

He is the lucky one. Now the other (arrow)! That's how it is done, friend. You have seen it.

542) *Ama abaya ama damitu, damitu isimoi arotu. Tai abaya. Ama ihi!*

Now my brother-in-law (will shoot the other arrow), the sister's husband who is the owner of the ritual clarinete. He get's ready. "It's your turn!"

543) *Ama sina? Ama ihi, ihi yakera! Hahinae, aka koyá. Tuatane hese, maraisa.*

"Now whose turn is it?" "It's your turn, you are good at it!" He took (the bell) away from him and fastened it on his leg. Right like this, friend.

544) *Ekuya hese, emo nakanaha. Orimahaya, inaré tane, inaré tane hese! Ariana, orabakaya.*([57])

That's how it works exactly, we won't be wrong. Fall in line, quietly, without any haste! The third turn, and the fourth.

545) *Amaseke isana waranaha. Tai erokonaha. Ooo osei, osei, osei ehhh.*

Now the same, as I described before. This will not change, sending the arrow off.

546) *Orabakaya hohote. Ama Pai Paiyó orabakaya hese. Atae kwahasika, amaseke Jaime, (isimoi arotu).*

They dance four turns. They (sing) "Pai Paiyó," four times as well.

And again (the arrow) is propelled, this time by Jaime (the owner of the sacred flute).

547) *Mate Jaime idamoana. Damana dibuya: Jaime, ihi mate idamoana. Mate ihi idamoana.*

That was when Jaime was not old yet. Someone says: "Jaime, you are not old yet. You are not yet old."

548) *Kwana, kwana, kwana! Kwana hatanu! Tamaha Jaime anoibana kwarika, Uboni anoibana ekida, taiseke anoibana taera.*

Forcefully, forcefully, forcefully! Toss the arrow forcefully! That Jaime is making a great effort, Uboni does not make an effort, but he (Jaime) makes a great effort.

549) *Hm, kwaiwitu. Barí, barí. Amayana mo eku. Tai isana waranaha monuka hese, maraisa.*

Hm, high up. And now (the arrow) comes down again. Afterwards they have it in their hands. The same way as I explained before, friend.

550) *Takore Pai Paiyó. Yewarane, maraisa.*

Then they whistle ("Pai Paiyó") again. Finishing up, friend.

---

[57] Shooting the arrows is part of the game of the "wild pig." They form two lines with one hand on the shoulder of the next man, coming closer and then moving away. One line represents "the people" and the other one wild pigs.

551) *Tamatika yewará. Ha tamaha eku nahanamu eku. Awahabara ebure sitaya.*

This game is finished. It is part of the nahanamu ritual. First the "wild pig" is imitated.

552) *Ebure sitakore nokabaya domu. Domu oreso. Dau. Hohonoko autu dahu ebotoroya, dau aroko isiko.*

When the imitation of the "wild pig" is finished, then comes the bird. It is (the imitation of) the "moriche" bird. A stick is placed in the middle of the dancing floor, a stick with leaves.

553) *Tatuka hau isia aru hisaba sanuka isia iridaha sabuka koyatane. Tatuka batokoya. Dau akahamana isia hohonoko autu tai hatabu daunona abanoko.*

There they tie up with moriche rope a piece of cooked sago. They hang it up on a treefork in the middle of the dancing floor where the arrow of the daunona figure had been.

554) *Tai tane. Ama dihana oko tai domu anahoro nahorokitane. Aromu... dau bomou tiaha isia. Tamaitane ts, ts, ts.*

That's that. Now we (imitate) a pecking bird. The bird... then with a long stick. Like that (sound of a pecking bird).

555) *Tuatane, kokotuka tuatane hese, sibahia, araisa, ariana sibahia. Motehomo isia tai aru dihana domu anahoro tekarla dihana.*

That way, everything the same way, they do a round, another one and a third round. With the fourth round people congregate where the sago is, the food for the bird.

556) *Tekariakore, aru nakaya, botoya sinarianaka. Tai domusita, domusita.*

When (the people) pile up, the sago falls to the ground, it breaks up into countless pieces. That's the imitation of the (moriche) bird, playing the bird.

557) *Ama homakaba sita, kaho yabasita. Amasabaya waraya kohu. Oko, ine mahokonamu, tamaha Winikinaraorakate waraya kaho.*([58])

Now comes the imitation of fishes, imitating the fishing of the "guabina" fish. Over there they say kohu. We here, where I come from, and also the people from Winikina, we say kaho.

558) *Kaho ayabasita. Tamaitane orimahaya, orimahae, besou. Orimahabuae.*

Performing the fishing of the "guabina." People link arms, they join (the two lines), and finish. They go on linking arms.

559) *Tai amoeku dabo ha, dabo sanuka. Damana kawanuka. Ama hoidu ahutu hakoma, hoidu ahutu hakoma .Hakoma anobaha behoro aso.*

One has a knife in his hand, a small knife. Another one something similar. Now, the line of the fishing rod is a moriche fiber string, a fiber string. The bait on the fishing line is some dogshit. (Antonio laughing)

560) *Behoro aso autuya koyá tane damana hiaka nobo, hiaka nobo anana hayama, hobahi araimo anautiaha horoheraha. Tai anobaha tane abaya.*

Sometimes the dogshit is fastened with a piece of old cloth, is seems there is a piece of old cloth, because it came from the mud completely dirty it was disgusting. This they put as bait (on the fishing rod).

561) *Dihana naruya. Sina kubatu aidamo? Sina yabatu aidamo? Ine yabatu aidamo. Seisa!*

They already leave. Who will be chief of the fish killers? Who will be chief of the fishermen? I will. Let's go then!

562) *Kaho yabaté, kaho yabaté, kaho yabaté! Naunahakotai moanaha, naunahakotai moanaha, moate amokomoko.*

They will be fishing "guabina," they fish "guabina." The one that doesn't go will fish nothing, he will be provided nothing, or will find a little.

---

[58] Guabina *Hoplias malabaricus*. Tirso Rivero pronounces kahu.

563) *Ahá, inekate naukitiné, ah, ah, amokomoko mamoakisá!*([59]) *Mamoakí sákatae amokomoko. Ihikate narú! Amokomoko kamoakisá ihikate naru, manobotomo arimá!*

Ah, I will go as well, ah, ah, I am getting small ones! It seems I am getting small ones only. "You will go as well!([60]) You go too so we will get small ones (at least), father of my children!"

564) *Inekate naute. Tatuma warao kohituma. Warao asida tubuya, tatuma yabamo warao kohituma.*

So I am going as well. These people are stingy. They are mean people, those fishermen are cheap.

565) *Amokomoko kamoate. Inekate mosibukai hamisá. Mahoidu ha, mosibukai ha, mabuarikate ha.*

They are giving only small (fish). Me too I have my fish hook. I have my fishing rod, my fish hooks, and I also have my machete (in order to clear the way).

566) *Dihana uhu isiko, maraisa. Uhu abaya, uhu tamaha tuatiaha abaya. Ya sibahia warao hakotai.*

You take a basket, friend. One carries a basket, a basket like this you have (showing a basket). The (fishermen) already do a round (the fish are sitting on the ground).

567) *Tuatane hese, maraisa. Orabakaya tane. Tamaha akanamunoko sibahia orabakaya nakakore, amaseke yabakitane.*

That's how it is, friend. They make four (rounds). Where they stop after four rounds, there they fish. (you hear a hissing sound of the moving fishing rods).

568) Heh, hidani! Hidani kabeso esowara hahenu! (words of the fishermen to the fishes).

"Hey, chief of the (guabina fish)! (hissing sound) Losen the string around your waist that your chief (carries)!"

---

[59] *Mamoakisá* for *mamoakitane*.

[60] Words of the man's wife. In this play the people are divided into fishermen and "guabina" fish.

569) *Heh, nokoae esowará. Kwa bohoyayama, bohoyayama, bohoyayama 'Daibuinabaka'.*

Heh, I heard you, the waist-string! The head (of the fish) appears, it seems, it appears in (the pool) Dauburunabaka, "Where-a-large-tree-fell."

570) *Hohubabaka bohoyayama, heh, nokoaene. Psst, hinokoae ine!*

(In the) "water-snake" (pool a fish head) appears, it seems, heh, I heard you. Psst, I heard you!

571) *Amawitu kwarimabakitane, mahara ahitakitane obononaha amawitu. Mahara hitakitane obononaha.*

Right now let's get a lot (of fish) out! my arm will not wear down now. My arm will not get tired.

572) *Heh, hidani kabeso obonobasa, komou, komou, komou. Kwarea komou, komou.*

Heh, guardian chief of (the guabina), the "Flat-bellies", here comes the bait. (sound of bait falling into the water) Further on bait is falling into the water.

573) *Ayamo anebukate yabaya, ekida. Tai hana wahatomá, ah, ekida. Tane witu.*

In front a man is fishing, nothing. This creek is empty already, ah, nothing. So it is.

574) *Turú tanakawitu hae. Oko ama kasaba? Ama hana tai mikí!*

Nothing is taking the bait. Where should we go now? Now we have a look at that creek over there!

575) *Kasaba? Tida mare ahana mikí! Tida mare. Tai yakera tai.*

Where? Let's have a look at the "merry woman" creek! The "merry woman."

That one is good (for fishing).

576) *Buhari kwakakore. Tai mate ihi minaha, maraisa. Tai ihi minaha.*

Somebody goes ahead clearing the way with a machete. That creek you have not seen, friend. That one you haven't seen.

577) *Buhari kwakaya, esokaya, aidamo hakotai. Ayamo anebu. Dihana tamaha hae, dihana tamaha, inaré tane.*

The headman cleans with a machete, clears the way, ahead of the men. He arrives already, and then another one arrives, all very poised.

578) *Hatekore kariá saí. Ha, nome hae! Inahitane([61]) amawitu kayu watubute.*

"There will be (fish," one can see fish) moving rapidly. "There is (fish)!" There really was. "Quiet! Right now we are filling our baskets."

579) *Tai tane sibahikomo, maraisa. Tai tamatika Warao ha, awere sibahine ha.*

Like this (they are talking), doing their rounds, [friend]. That's how these Warao are around here, doing their round close by.

580) *Hohonoko kobú. Atae nakakore, isana waranaha monuka, maraisa: Pst, hahi obonohase.([62])*

The dancing floor is full (of people). When they come again (to the same point), as I said before, friend: "Pst, moving (the tackle to call). Flat-belly."

581) *Se kabeso, kabeso! Se kabeso, kabeso! Hisowara hahenu! Hisowara hahenu! Hisowara hahenu! Hisowara hahenu! Amawitu bahikitane, dihana ine noherawitu.*

"That thing around your waist! Well, that thing! Losen the string, losen the waist-string! Right now we return, I am already quite hungry."

582) *Komou, komou. Dous, dous. Aiii, mabahanae! Amasaba dous, dous, mabahanae!*

Plas, plas (the bait falls). (The fish) sounds. "Aiii (shout), (The 'guabina' fish) caught my bait!" Now over there: "(the fish) is catching the bait!"

583) *Ah, ah, nome era, nome era! Damana dabo hakotai, tai dabo! Dihana mobaha tamatika nakakore, kabataya dihana.*

Ah, ah, there are really many ('guabina' fish). Somebody (among the fish people) has a knife, that knife! He already cuts the bait as it falls (on the water).

---

[61] For *inaré tane*.

[62] For *obonobasa*.

584) *Ah, kabatanae, kabatanae. Dawa monikatae. Dawa monikatae, dawa monikatae.*

Ah, he cut it, he cut it. The son-in-law will have problems (as he brings no fish). The son-in-law has problems (no fish and a fish-hook lost).

585) *Mosibukai, mosibukai kabatanae! Hae cará! Mosibukai yakeraha. Sa, tiarone mosibukai araisa ha.*

"My fish-hook, my fish-hook is cut lose! There, devil! My fish-hook was a good one. Doesn't matter, I have another fish-hook!

586) *Araisa ha, mosibukai ha, kauyabate. Makasiatane, asamatane kauyabate. Mabua hakore, mabua sabanaha, hai! Hai, hai, koyá, koyá!*

There is another fish-hook and I am tying it, quickly and poorly tying it (to the fishing rod). Taking off a piece from my old loincloth, zass! Zass, zass, and it is [tied] (on the rod)!"

587) *Araya yemarakore. Asamatane yemaraene bahamá! Hau isia yemarakore dibuhidaha kabatanae.*

Then he ties it (to the fish-hook). "As I tied (the bait) poorly, (the fish) caught it!" When it is tied with moriche fiber, it is easy to cut it.

588) *Tamaha kaho ahi ihido, kaho yabakitane. Hau isia yemaranaha. Awai ahidotihi, yemarakitane hiaka nobo.*

When one fishes 'guabina', it has very sharp teeth. One shouldn't tie (the bait) with moriche fiber. Since its name is 'sharp', one should tie it with an old piece of cloth.

589) *Hiaka nobo yemarakorekotai, tai dihana abukore kabatanaha. Butí tane nakaya, ahi sotó, sotó tia.*

When one ties (the fish-hook) with [that] old cloth, when (the fish) bites it can't cut through it. (The cloth) is pulled to pieces, (but) the teeth remain buried.

590) *Hau yemarae kabatanae dihana. Yakara dihana. Ya yemarae hi yewará.*

When he tied it up with moriche fiber, right then is was cut. But now it is alright. He tied it up and finished.

591) *Dihana kaho yabaya. Ah, kwarika kubaya. Kwarika kubaya, naburuae. Dihana marako wabae.*

They are already fishing "guabinas".Ah, they are killing ever more (fish). They kill (fish) in heaps. Already the catch is dying.

592) *Materá? Mate, mate. Mate, mate. Mate sanukawitu turá! Mate! Ya, ya, ya! Dihana ya, kayu watubuae.*

"Still more?" "Yes, some more, some more. Still a little more! Keep going just a little bit! More! Now stop! Already enough, the basket is full.

593) *Mayu uhu autuya, yakera tai dihana. Ateho kawahera tubuyatihi, tuatane nahorotené! Damana hakotai uhukobu, damana uhu akohoya.*

My basket is half full, that's enough already. As the (guabina) has a long body, I am going to eat a lot! Somebody has a full basket, another one's basket is almost full.

594) *Damana ahowetehemo uhukobu. Damana uhu autuya. Dihana yakera, dihana seisa!*

Somebody lucky has a full basket. Another one has his basket half full. That's enough already, let's go!

595) *Ya dihana dabaituma noho wabaya. Ah, dabai marabai noho wabayané. Marabai noho wabayané, que vaina! Marabai noho wabayaha.*

Our mothers-in-law are dying from hunger. Ah, my mother-in-law is on the verge of dying from hunger! My mother-in-law is dying from hunger, what a drag! My mother-in-law is in a state of breakdown [from hunger].

596) *Seisa dihana, tamaha kahobahi kahanoko tamatikawituana! Ote sabuka misá! Tatukawituana misá!*

Let's go! This here is not really our land and village! We are quite far away! We are not close yet!

597) *Wayaba sabuka! Dihana seisa! Tamaha kahokohi nawarawaranae tia. Ya karawaituma kawakaya.*

"Let's finish up now! Let's go! The sun is already declining. Our mothers-in-law are waiting for us.

598) *Dihana seisa! Ahabaramokotai eburihi kabakitane! Karabaituma kebesaba hekunu nautakitane!*

Let's go now! The ones ahead (should sound) [hitting] the sangrito roots (so that those at home hear us coming) and our mothers-in-law start to kindle the fires!"

599) *Aru hakore, imahakitane, dihana oko nahorokitane. Eh, dihana nahoro-kitane!*

If there is sago, they should make tortillas, so that we should eat. "Hey, come to eat right away!"

600) *Dokohotu, dokohotu, eburihi hese. Dokohotu eburihikaba. Eburihikaba dokohotu.*

They shout and shout banging the roots of the sangrito. Gritando and striking the root of the sangrito (tree). They strike and shout.

601) *Hekunu, hekunu! hanoko awere nakakore. Ah, hekunu, hekunu! dokohotu. Ah, hekunu, hekunu! hanokoarao nokokore.*

They shout "fire, fire!", when they come close to the house. They shout "fire, fire!" "Fire, fire!" when the people in the house can hear them.

602) *Hekunuyama dabaituma, hekunu nautakotu! Dabaituma nautubukotu.*

The mothers-in-law should light the fire, they tell them to light the fires. "Mothers-in-law, light the fires!"

603) *Heh, hekunu dibuhida*([63])*, moho dibuhida! Dahi oriwakaya, dahi araisa oriwakaya. Dahi araisa oriwakaya, dahituma kokotuka oriwakaya.*

"Heh, quick the fire, with speedy hands!" One father-in-law is glad, and so is another one. Another father-in-law is glad too, all fathers-in-law are glad.

604) *Tahutuma oriwakaya, nobotomo kokotuka oriwakaya. Dihana homakaba naoya. Ebisaba dabaituma hekunu nautubuae. Mate tai, mate!*

---

[63] Antonio makes an effort to use the more authentic (in morichalero terms) *dubuhi-da*. Tirso Rivero insists on *dibuhida* (in modern terms).

The women are glad, all the children are glad. Fish is already arriving. This very moment the mothers-in-law light the fire. Just a minute, wait!

605) *Heh doró, dauwa awahabara. Ariatuka dawa hese, ariatuka dawa hese, ariatuka dawa hese. Eh, eh, uhu kwatubuae diá.*

The first son-in-law appears already, and so does the next one, and the next, and so on. Eh, eh, the basket is full already (observe the children).

606) *Tamaha uhu autuya, tamaha uhu autuya, damana uhu kwatubuae, ahowetemo. Ah, tuaraya diahana.*

This basket is half full, this one is half full, another one is full, he was lucky. Ah, they already are resting.

607) *Sanuka tuaraya, atida tatuka tuaraya. Amasaba tuaraya, amasaba tuaraya. Ah, ekida, monikatae ine, mosibukai kabatanae.*

They rest a little, the wife there rests a little. There they rest, over there they also rest. Ah, nothing, I will have a quarrel because my fish-hook severed.

608) *Mate hisaka yabayakorese, hisaka abane natokoya obonoyakorese, mosibukai seún.*

Already before beginning to fish, even before getting the first catch, my fishhook went (the husband tells his wife).

609) *Maharako ekidakotai tamaha manamo uatokonaine. Ateho kawahera-tihi, tuatane nahorotekó, matida, manobotomo arani.*

Without any catch, I finally got those two (guabinas). Since they are large ones, you are going to eat, my wife, mother of my children.

610) *Nahorotekó. Marabai saba konaru wari hisaka. Orisaba nisanu! Orisaba nisanu, marabai kware konaru.*

You will be eating. Take a large (fish) to my mother-in-law!Take (the other fish) for yourself! Take one for you and bring the other to my mother-in-law.

611) *Marabai marahi isiko korú takunarae. Nahorokunarae, tatamo oko obononaha. Orisaba nisanu.*

My mother- and father-in-law should eat with it, They should have to eat, we don't want anything from over there. Take the rest for yourself.

612) *Orisaba nisaya, mohorekokore, mohoreko arai mohabasikore, warao hisakakore, orisaba nisanu!*

They fished for everybody, if there are ten, or fifteen, or if there are twenty, take for everybody (this is part of the game)!

613) *Asibia, uhu asibiakore, araniyata konaruya, tata arani nahorokitane.*

(In another hut) they might have half a basket, if there is half a basket, they take it to their mother, so that she can eat.

614) *Tata arani wahabukitane, tata are nahorokitane. Naruá dani tamaha dihana.*

There their mother will roast (the fish), so they have to eat. (The woman) left (to hand) it to her mother.

615) *Tamaha hiabitu dihana, atae tamaha ine orisaba nisanaha dihana daní, nahoro dihana idamo isiko, wahabutane nahoro.*

"This is for you. I devided it up for you (lit. for each other), mother, for you and my old father to eat it roasted."

616) *Abita orisaba nisanaetihi tai dihana anobotomo isiko anibora isiko. Nahoroya dihana.*

Because it was gotten for all one by one, as well for the children as for the spouse. Already they are eating.

617) *Amate dabaiyata tata nahoroya dihana. Tai dabai dahi nahoroya. Tatamo konanaha dihana.*

Over there at the mother-in-law's house they are eating already. That mother- and father-in-law are eating. It is brought from over there.

618) *Ama erawitu hakore kokotuka konaruya dabaiyata. Dabai wahabuya kokotuka, diri arai wahabuya. Diri wahabuya yewará, tatamo autuya abane uhu ekuhese, aukwatida kware toaya.*

Now, if there is a lot, it is taken to the mother-in-law. She will roast it all, on a barbecue she will roast it. When she finishes roasting, she puts half away in a basket for her daughter (sending the father-in-law).

619) *Tamaha dihana hiharako, hiharakotihi. Yakera dima, asibia hisaba nisanaera? Tatuka nahorokitane.*

"This is your catch. Because it is your catch." "Very well, father. Did you keep half of it?" Now to eat!

620) *Tamahakotai oriwaka emo, maraisa. Bietayanarone, tai tamaha sitayaha. Kahoyaba asita.*

This all is (a digression) besides the feast, friend. Even if it would not be part of the fiesta, this is imitating the fishing of the "guabina."

621) *Ama nokaba, tamaha nokabaya, yewarakore nokabaya, muhotosita, maraisa, muhotosita.*

A little afterwards, after this finishes, a little later, there is the imitation of the "busco" fish, friend, the play of the "busco" fish.

622) *Tairakate ha tamaha nahanamu eku. Takore tamatuma sitanaha. Ine maobonona emo.*

This is also part of the nahanamu fiesta (but not part of the ritual). Nevertheless, they don't imitate the "busco" fish. I don't like (the dance of the "busco" fish).

623) *Eburewitu sitaya. Ebure sitaya yewarate, nokabaya, nokabaya sitate domu, nokabaya sitate kaho.*

The very dance of the wild pig we perform. When that dance is over, we imitate the moriche" bird, when that is done, we imitate the "guabina" fish.

624) *Kaho yabate, nokabayakotai sitate tamahakotai muhoto, muhoto.*

When the fishing the "guabina" is over, then there is the imitation of the "busco," the "busco morichalero" fish.([64])

---

[64] There are two varieties of "busco." Here the talk is of the "busco morichalero" (*Hoplosternum littorale*).

625) *Ihi hisaka miae o minaha? Tai muhoto tuatane hese, maraisa. Kahoyaba tuatane hese, maraisa.*

You have seen it once or not? That "busco" fish is like that, friend. Fishing "guabina" is similar.

626) *Tane Warao orimahaya, horo, tamatuatiaha horo, yawihi nobotuma siakaya.*

People link arms again (again in two rows), and heap up old temiche leaves.

627) *Siakaya, siakaya kokotuka, siakaya, siakaya yewará.*

They heap up (the leaves on the "busco" people), heap up and finish.

628) *Tai dihana isana waranaha monuka, maraisa. Isana monuka hese. Tai naruya kubatu aidamo.*

This is as I told you before, friend, exactly like before. There goes the chief of those that slay (fish).

629) *Sina kubatu aidamo? Ine kubatu aidamo, seisa!*

Who will be chief of the fishermen? I will be chief of the fishermen, let's go!

630) *Dihana naruya. Sibahia, sibahia, araisa, ariana, orabakaya. Dihana tamaha tabí, tamaha tabí.*

They are already leaving. They do a round, another round, a third and a fourth. That (dance) is progressing already, is advancing.

631) *Mate inahera, ah, anoko sebuhukí, anoko sebuhukí. Sebuhukí tei tei tei tei tí, nokokí! Ah no, inahera.*

Nothing can be heard, the spot must be pushed down pushed down (to kill the fish by jumping on the leaves). Let's push (the movement of pushing), listen! Ah, nothing can be heard.

632) *Seisa! Kwarea! Kasaba? Tai ahabara aidamo buhari oaya, ahabara, ayamo anebu.*

Let's go! Faster! Where? This first chief gets hold of his machete, him first and after him his men.

633) *Kokotuka isana waranaha monuka hese, maraisa. Naruí, sibahia. Arianatane, orabakaya Atae nokokitane, dihana tamahá.*

Everything as I explained before, friend. They left and do a round.([65]) A third round and then a fourth, listening again and that's it.

634) *Kasabukaha? Tamá dawa idamo amuhu. dawa idamo amuhu, ahibaka.*

Which one? (There is the pond) "bone of the first son-in-law".([66]) (And the pond where there are termites): "bone of the first son-in-law", and "termites."

635) *Mate nokokí. Inaitane, inaitane, nokokí mate. Hong, hong, hong, koitaya wakataha ihi. Koitayakatá, koitayakatá. Tamaha yanara?*

Vamos a escuchar. Tranquilo, tranquilo, vamos a escuchar. Hong, hong, hong, (sound the fishes), You are making a noise, it seems. I think you are making a noise, you are making a noise. Isn't that so?

636) *Sanuka ahanoko sebuhukí! Burae, burae, burae, burae, di, di, di, di, di; tok, tok, tok, tok, tok.*

Let's kick the cover a little! They jump and jump and jump, di, di, di, di, di (the sound on the leaves); tok, tok, tok, tok, tok (the sound of the fishes breathing).

637) *Atae araisatane. Kwana sabuka sebuhukí! Amaseke anabukarina, eh, eh, nabutunae!*

Again another one (jumping). Let's kick (them) a little harder! Now (the fishes) are going to escape, eh, eh, they already are getting away!

638) *Oho dawa idamo amuhu nome kwatae, oho ahibaka. Oho wahatoma, tai aobonona tamate obonone mohoro. Sé, moho dibuhida. Moho dibuhida ahabara.*

The pond "bone of the first son-in-law" really exploded, the termite pond, yes. Oho didn't produce anything, if we had only come here first! Now, a quick hand (to gather the fishes). First thing to have a quick hand.

---

[65] The "people" form an outer ring on the dancing platform, while the "fishes" are in the middle, half covered by the leaves.

[66] "Bone of the black heron." Mythical language for the principal son-in-law.

639) *Akoho tatuka isibutu ha, arani. Kabatae dihana. Kabatakore, haii, arianakotai mahanewitu.*

There is an electric eel at the rivermouth, the origin.([67]) They cut (the ground). When they cut it, haii (sound of cutting), the next time (they cut) very close.

640) *Oi, mate! Tamaha motehomo mahanewitu, mahanewitu, mahanewitu, mahanewitu. Oi!*

Watch out! Wait! (The fourth time) they cut very close, very, very close. Watch out!

641) *Oi, amawitu bahekí! Tamatika isibutu hakotai, ahabara tatuka nakayakore, saraya dihana. Saraya.*

Watch out! Let's now go home (with the fish)! When one first arrives, that eel there gives you an electric shock. It attacks.

642) *Tín sará. Akae! Akae! Ariatuka anebu hakotai kwai kobukaha waha yata. Tamaha muhotosita, maraisa. Tamaha kokotuka dihana.*

The shock hits you. Help! Help! Another man helps him up and to the shore. This is the play of the "busco" fish, friend. That's all.

643) *Tamaha aukwa dihana. Ebure asita, domu oreso asita, kahu ayabasita, muhoto akubasita.*

That's the end already. Playing the wild pig, the moriche bird, fishing "guabina," and slaying "busco morichalero."

644) *Ebure asita, domu oreso asita, kahu ayabasita, muhoto akubasita, orabakaya. (Ama mutemoikitane, mutemohiyaha).*

Playing the wild pig, the moriche bird, fishing "guabina," and slaying "busco," four (dances).

(This is during the day; now starts the game "blowing over the eyes", this is after nightfall).

---

[67] *Arani*, the "mother" or origin of the species.

645) *Tamate kokotuka dihana. Amasike tihidamo, wayaba takitane. Tai dihana abesona.*

That's all. Now (comes) the old woman, to be pushed around. That's the end already.

646) *Dihana tamaha, tamatika tamaha, hoho, nahanamu ahoho. Dihana ekoroya monuka, tiarone mate ekoronaha.*

This is (the dance of) the nahanamu (ritual), the dance, the ritual dance of the sago container. It is as if (the ritual) would end, but it still does not end.

647) *Mate amasike tidaidamo mutemoikitane. Tamaha ihi obonoya mohoro? Tai daisa abanaha, tai abaya ahabara ikanamunae, dokotu awaratu.*

Now comes the old woman "to blow over the eyes." Perhaps this is what you would like (to hear)? One doesn't have to look for another (woman), you take the one that first got up, the singer (wife of the "owner of the sacred clarinete.")

648) *Taihese. Isana waranaha kotai, yewarakore nahoroya dihana, yewará. Nahoro yewará, imananí.*

Herself. As I said before, when they finish they eat. They finished (eating). They finished the meal and night fell.

649) *Dihana tihidamo ahiaka nisaya, tamaisia kabukida abaya. Ateho, tamatikamo ateho kokotuka diaka.*

The old woman already takes a dress, a very short dress. Her body, from here on her whole body is outside.([68])

650) *Tamasia abaya, nasi koyaya, nasi koyaya, tamasia koyaya, tamasia koyaya. Ahabara tai anibora.*

She puts it on and also dons adornments (like necklaces), she puts them here and there. First goes her husband (behind her).

---

[68] She is partially naked.

651) *Keoboyaha, amasaba hohonoko keoboyaha. Hanoko ekumo ehoboyaha, hohonoko arai abayaha.*

They arrive, arrive at the dancing floor. They leave the house and position themselves on the (dancing) platform.

652) *Kawará, uriabane kawaraya. Uriabane kawarakore tamatika oko nebusike tamatika. Terén, tatukamo kawaraya, terén araisatane.Terén ariana, terén orabakaya.*

The step ahead, and walk slowly. As they walk slowly, the men are standing around. The little bell chimes([69]), and rings a second time. Ding, a third time; ding, (it sounds) a fourth time.

653) *Tatuka nebu manamo kanamuya, nebu orabakaya. Taisi bahia. Mate inaré tane, terén.*

Then two or four men get up. They turn around towards her. They still won't talk, ding.

654) *Terén, terén, terén, terén. Hisaka, tuatane hese. Ayamo araisa, tuatane hese ariana, orabakaya. Amaseke tamatika dokohotoya. Dokohotoya saba waraya. Oi, aba warate. Kanobo hi nokoya!*

Ding, ding, ding, ding. One round, the same way. After that another (round), likewise a third, and a fourth one. Right then (the woman) starts singing. She sings and they tell her: "Watch out not to sing badly. The kanobo spirit is hearing you."

655) *Aba waranaka. Ihi musaberara? Musaba kanukidakore masaba waranu! Ah, tamaitane dokohotu, amatane dokohotu.([70])*

"Don't sing badly, you remember? If you don't remember, tell me." Ah, such is the song, That's the song.

656) *Ote hanokoarao ohóóó, ohóóó! Naruya, naruya araisa. Tatuka nakakore, atae dokohotoya.*

---

[69] A ritual bell, called *nasi tehere*.

[70] The song, *noakukubuté, noakukubuté*: 'someone got lost in the forest'.

Far away in the house they wistle. She goes and does another round (on the dancing floor). When she arrives (at the start), she sings again.([71])

657) *Noakukubuté. Manamo, ariana tuatane hese, maraisa. Ama tamaha dibuya hanoko arao, ama ariana dokohotukitia.*

Someone got lost in the forest. Twice and a third time, friend. Now the people from the house speak: "Now, she is going to sing the third round."

658) *Tuatane hese dokohotoya: Noakukubuté. Dihanamo. Sibahia, orabakaya. Tuatane hese noakukubuté waraya orabakaya.*

Likewise she sings: Someone got lost in the forest. Three rounds. She turns around, four. Likewise she sings four times "someone lost in the woods."

659) *Tai orabakaya warakore, ama hisaka, neburatu hisaka tamasaba nakaya, sanuka tamasabaú tane. Ihi miae.*

When she has sung four times, then one of the young men steps forward a little bit further. You have seen it.

660) *(The woman blows over the boys eyes, so he won't get lost in the woods). Ama sibahia, tamasaba naruya. Asabahimo. Asabahimo sina? Agostina! Agostina.*

Now (the woman) does a round and arrives there (at the young man). (Four women) crack jokes (from the house). Who is cracking jokes? Agostina! Agostina (is cracking jokes).

661) *Agostina, araisa! Yatu orisabahikitane yakera, naokotu! Naokotu, tai tihidamo bahikitane, tihidamo sabahikitane!*

Agostina, another one! Come on, insult each other well! Come and insult that old woman, fight with that old woman!

662) *Tahutuma dihanamo o orabakaya tidaidamo sabahikitane. Ama tamatikamo naruya, tihidamo naruaya, terén, terén.*

Three or four fight with the old woman. Now then the old woman goes (to where the men are), the woman walks, ding, ding.

---

[71] In the middle of the platform are four young men with their heads covered with a cloth or shirt, looking towards the east. The woman leaves the house and walks slowly towards them. Then she does a turn around them (counter-clockwise).

663) *Tamatika neburatu diboto nakaya. Diboto kanamune, dibuya kahurukomo, terén, terén, terén:*

Here the young man stops in front of her. When he stops in front of her, he says, jumping here and there, ding, ding:

664) *Hebu mikorakora, hebu mikorakora, hebu mikorakora, hebu mikorakora!*

"Don't look at the hebu-spirit, don't look at the hebu-spirit, don't look at him, don't look at him!"

665) *Tane takore, ama tahutuma, awarao hakotai, dibuya, arakobo sanuka hakore, auka hakore: Dakobo sanuka mia!*

When he does this, the women, being relatives, speak. If it is a little brother or son (Agostina speaks): "Little brother, look!

666) *Tai tidaidamó, tai tidaidamó kohí, tai tidaidamo nohoida. Dakobo sanuka mia!*

That old woman, she is cheap, that old woman is starving. Little brother, look!

667) *Dakobo sanuka warao taraha tamaha. Moo akabatu tamaha. Osibu akubatu tamaha.Bisi akabatu tamaha dakobo sanuka.*

This little brother is a hard worker. He cuts (old moriche palms) for grubs. He slays morocoto fish. He cuts down chachicamo trees (to make canoes), that little brother.

668) *Tidaidamó dakobo sanuka miané. Tidaidamo sabayaha. Tamaha yewaraya, sibahia, Ah no!*

The old woman is looking at the little brother. They are quarreling with the old woman. This (game) ends, they turn around, Ah no!

669) *Tamaha tane dibakore, tatuka ama tahutuma sabasaba baria. Wayabá! Tane maraisa.*

When they stopped quarreling, (the singer) turned to the women. Go far away! That's how it is, friend.

670) *Wayabá, wayabá, wayabá! Orabakaya. Ama tahutuma orabakaya hakotai: "Tidaidamó, kasabasaba ahara wiyá sané!*

Go away, go away, go away! Four times. Now those four women (say): "Old woman, don't pull our arms!"

671) *Ahara basabasaú, tidaidamo ahara basabasa.*[72] *Tai tidaidamo, tidaidamo nohoida. Tai tidaidamo dokoida. Tai tidaidamo hainone.*

"The old woman has thin arms, thin arms she has. That old woman is starving. That old woman has a big mouth. That old woman is gluttonous.

672) *Tai tidaidamo mooi. Tai tidaidamo aru simorokoida. Awarao hakotai tidaidamo sabahia Tane maraisa.*

That old woman likes moriche grubs. That old woman likes brown (old) sago starch." Her relatives quarrel with the old woman. That's how it is.

673) *Orabakaya hakore, orabakaya yakera. Kwarika tanaha. Tai tatuka isimoi arotu ha dihana, isimoi arotu ha.*

If there are four women (fighting), four is fine. More (than four) is no good. In this moment the owner of the sacred clarinete appears, the owner of the sacred clarinete is there.

674) *Orabakaya yakera dihana, dihana tidaidamo wabohitaya dihana. Tatukamo naruya hatabu inaruya, hatabu. Hatabu oró, tatuka tidaidamo yaroya.*

Four (women) is enough, already the old woman is getting tired. After that they go to shoot the arrow, the arrow. (The clarinete player) sets the arrow up and the old woman (his wife) arrives.

675) *Nebu kanamukotu! Nebu kanamuya. Turá, turá, turá. Tane asibahine kotai, sibahinú.*

Boys, get up! and the men are getting up. They get up, and up they get. Thus (the old woman) did a round (by the arrow and the boys), did a round.

676) *Hatabu awere turá. Isimoi koitaya: dé, dé, dé, dé, dedere dé. Abesona-witu, yewaranae dihana.*

Near the arrow she stops. The clarinte sounds: dé, dé, dé, dé, dedere dé. The very end, (the dance is) finished.

---

[72] Literally, flat.

677) *Ama tatukamo tida hisaka hanokeku ha. Ihi nokoae. Uriabane konaruya.*

Now a single woman is still in the house. (To his wife): "You heard it." (The flutist) slowly leads (the singer) away.

678) *Hanoko awere denokoya: Ihi musabera? Musabera? Musaberakore musabera. Oi, oi monite, hinokoya.*

Close to the house he asked: "Do you remember? Remember? You certainly must remember. Watch out not to bother (the kanobo spirit), he is hearing you.

679) *Naruya, naruya, tamaha dokohotoya. Mianaká, hisaka, araisa mianaká. Sanuka kawarakomo, maraisa.*

They walk, they walk, that (old woman) is singing. Look at me, the first, the second (round), look at me." They walk a little stopping here and there, friend.

680) *Ariana, mianaká. Tamaha motehomo ayahu, maraisa. Mianaká, tamatika dibuya, tamatika dibuya:Sina hoa yamanae? Damitu hoa yamanae.*

The third (round), "look at me." This is the end of the fourth finger (the fourth round)."Look at me," (the old woman) sings: "Who killed me with hoa incantations? My brother-in-law killed me with hoa incantations."([73])

681) *Ine hoa yahinaene. Ine hoarotu iné. Tamaitane amu soa soa soa. Ayawarana dihana. Nahanamu ekoronae.*

(Another woman sings:) "I did cut you down, I am a hoarotu shaman." This way (the other woman) blows over her eyes huh huh huh. Here it ends, the nahanamu dance is over. (The old woman disappears in the forest. That's all, friend. This is around 9 pm.)

682) *Ine wahi arokohotu naminanaha. Ine konehoida hisaba warakomoni.*

The song of the howler monkey I don't know. I cannot tell you lies.([74])

(End of Antonio Lorenzano's narrative.)

---

[73] ZH, ms; in this case the woman has no *damitu* and is not male anyway. In Warao one sings frequently the role of an opposite sex person.

[74] Almost at midnight a select group of *wisiratu* shamans gather on the dancing floor and sing the song of the howler monkey. (The narrator, however, is a *bahanarotu* shaman.)

Wahi Arokohotu

by Segundo Rivero, Antonio's *natoro* (grand-son).

683) *Wahi isia, tai kanobo arokohotu; nahanamuwitu isia dokotu waraya.*

Regarding (the song of) the howler monkey: During the proper nahanamu ritual this chant is sung.

684) *Habi sanuka isia waranaha. Wahi isia kokotuka dokotu waraya, hohonoko witu arai.*

It is not sung during the habi sanuka (fertility rites). During the (the song of) the howler monkey all (of a group of men) sing the chant, on the very dancing platform.

685) *Ama wisatu tai dokotu anaminatu waraya warao isiko. A las 11 de la noche empieza y termina a las 12, medianoche.*

At this time the wisiratu-shaman who knows the song sings together with the men. They start at 11pm. and end at 12 midnight.

686) *Kokotuka oreku dokotu waraya sentados alrededor en el medio. Dokotu awaratu aidamo autuwitu ha, duhaya.*([75])

All sing together the chant, sitting in a circle in a round (on the dancing platform). The elder who knows the chant is in the middle, sitting down.

687) *Dokotu awaraya, waraya. Hetoyaha takore, kanamuya. Dan la vuelta. Dan cuatro vueltas. Hanoko etokoya, araisa etokoya.*

They sing and sing. When they went on (singing for some time)([76]), they get up (and walk in a circle on the platform).([77]) They do four rounds.

---

[75] Instead of *duhuya*.

[76] A task still ahead is to translate the chant together with bilingual native speakers of Warao and Ye'kwana.

[77] They walk around the *hohonoko* dancing platform (counter-clockwise) in a circle. Then the representation of the howler monkey starts (*wahi sitakitane*).

688) *Hanoko etokoya, araisa etokoya.*

They rattle at the house posts, and then at another (house).

689) *Ayahu dihana kokotuka yewaranae. Ama nakokitane. Nako yewarakore, ahiaka kabeyataya. Dihana ubakitane! Aheku nakaya, ubakitane.*

At the end, everything is finished. Now on for a bath! When the bath is finished, we undress. Now to sleep! Around the fireplace we get to sleep.

690) *Tai dihana kokotuka. Aukwa.*

This is all already. The end!

BIBLIOGRAPHY

Acosta Saignes, Miguel. [1954] 1961. *Estudios de la etnología antigua de Venezuela*. Caracas: Universidad Central de Venezuela.

Barral, Basilio de. 1964. *Los indios Guaraúnos y su cancionero: historia, religión y alma lírica*. Biblioteca "Missionalia Hispánica", Vol. 15. Madrid: Concejo Superior de Investigaciones Científicas, Departamento de Misionología Española.

Colón, Cristóbal. 1989. *Textos y documentos completos. Prólogo y notas de Consuelo Varela.* Madrid: Alianza Universidad.

Gassón, Rafael & Dieter Heinen. 2008. *Is there a generic Warao? Key issues in the ethnography and historical ecology of the Orinoco Delta.* Paper presented at the Conference of the Society for the Anthropology of Lowland South America, Oxford, 17-21 June.

Gumilla, José. [1741] 1993. *El Orinoco Ilustrado y Defendido*. Vol. 68. Caracas: Biblioteca de la Academia Nacional de la Historia (BANH).

Harcourt, Robert.[1613] 1967. *A Relation of a Voyage to Guiana*. The Hakluyt Society. Edited by Sir C. Alexander Harris. Nendeln: Kraus Reprint Limited.

Heinen, H. Dieter & Julio Lavandero. 1973. Computación del Tiempo en dos Subtribus Warao. *Antropológica* 35: 12-13.

Heinen, H. Dieter & Kenneth Ruddle. 1974. Ecology, Ritual, and Economic Organization in the Distribution of Palm Starch among the Warao of the Orinoco Delta. *Journal of Anthropological Research* 30: 116-38.

Heinen, H. Dieter, Werner Wilbert and Tirso Rivero. 1999. *IDAMO KA-BUKA El viejo corto*. Caracas: Fundación La Salle, pp. 107.

Herrmann, Stefanie. 2007. Perspektiven auf die Waraosprache und das Waraosprechen. Unpublished Doctoral Dissertation. Marburg: Philipps-University.

Keymis, Lawrence. [1596] 1968. *A Relation of the Second Voyage to Guiana, Perfourmed and Written in the Yeare 1596*. New York: Da Capo. (No page numbers, some letters are used.)

Lavandero, Julio. 1986. Mundo Guarao: Ka nonatu Dioso, karani. Nuestro Creador, nuestra madre. *Venezuela Misionera* (año 47) 531: 72-7.

Lavandero Pérez, Julio. 1994. *Uaharaho, ethos narrativo (III)*. Caracas: Ediciones Paulinas.

Lavandero, Julio & H. Dieter Heinen. 1986. Canciones y bailes del ritual de la Nouara. *Montalbán* 17:199-243.

Loukotka, Cestmír. 1968. *Classification of South American Indian Languages*. Edited by J. Wilbert. Los Angeles: University of California.

Ojer, Pablo. 1966. *Formación del Oriente Venezolano: Creación de las gobernaciones*. Caracas: Universidad Católica Andrés Bello.

Ralegh, Walter. [1596] 1848. *The Discoverie of the Large, Rich and Bewtitvl Empire of Gviana*. London: Hakluyt Society.

Rale[i]gh, Sir Walter. [1596] 1986. *El descubrimiento del grande, rico y bello imperio de Guayana*. Traducción de Antonio Requena. Caracas: Ediciones Juvenal Herrera.

Roth, Walter ([1924] 1970). *An Introductory Study of the Arts, Crafts, and Customs of the Guiana Indians*. New York: Johnson Reprint Corporation.

Ruddle, Kenneth R. 1977. *"Sago in the New World" in The First International Sago Symposium: The Equatorial Swamp as a Natural Resource*. Edited by Koonlin Tan. Kuala Lumpur:Kemajuan Kanji, pp.53-64.

Suárez, M. Matilde. 1968. *Los Warao*. Caracas: IVIC.

Varela, Consuelo. 1989. (Ver Colón)

Wilbert, Johannes. 1996. *Mindful of Famine: Religious Climatology of the Warao Indians*. Cambridge: Harvard University Press.

Ethnologische Studien
hrsg. von Ulrich Köhler (Universität Freiburg)

Ulrich Köhler (Hg.)
Nueva Maravilla
Eine junge Siedlung im Kontext massiver indianischer Migration nach San Cristobál de la Casas, Chiapas, Mexiko

Um 1975 begann ein Prozeß massiver Immigration von Indianern nach San Cristóbal, die 35-40 eigene Siedlungen gründeten mit zus. über 30.000 Einwohnern. Eine davon ist Nueva Maravilla. Viele Siedlungen wurden von aus ihren Heimatdörfern vertriebenen Protestanten mit religiösem Bezug angelegt oder entstanden durch Landbesetzungen von Anhängern der EZLN. Nueva Maravilla wurde demgegenüber 1995 von fünf Tzotzil-Indianern wie ein Wirtschaftsbetrieb gegründet und entwickelt. Das hat schon in wenigen Jahren zu erstaunlichen Ergebnissen geführt. Nueva Maravilla ist eine aufstrebende Siedlung, alles andere als ein Slum.

Bd. 37, 2005, 448 S., 39,90 €, gb., ISBN 3-8258-8315-9

LIT Verlag Berlin – Münster – Wien – Zürich – London
Auslieferung Deutschland / Österreich / Schweiz: siehe Impressumsseite

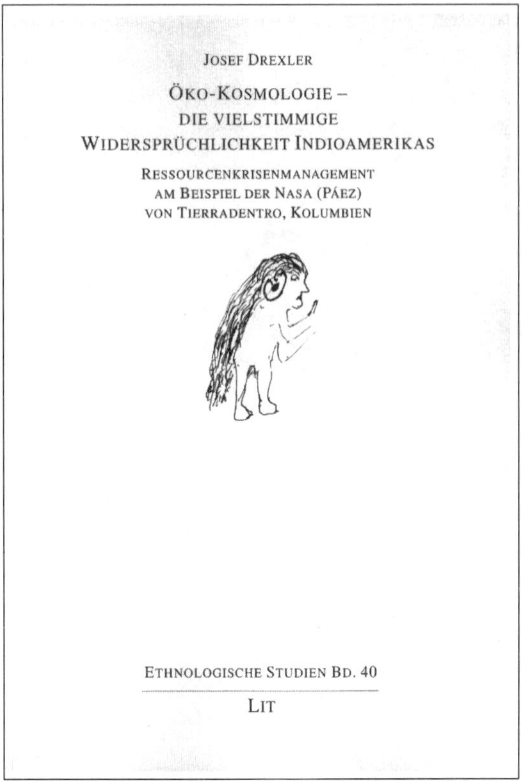
JOSEF DREXLER
ÖKO-KOSMOLOGIE –
DIE VIELSTIMMIGE
WIDERSPRÜCHLICHKEIT INDIOAMERIKAS
RESSOURCENKRISENMANAGEMENT
AM BEISPIEL DER NASA (PÁEZ)
VON TIERRADENTRO, KOLUMBIEN
ETHNOLOGISCHE STUDIEN BD. 40
LIT